DAILY READINGS
— FROM —
ThinkBetter
LiveBetter

Also by Joel Osteen

Break Out!
Break Out! Journal
Daily Readings from Break Out!
Every Day a Friday
Every Day a Friday Journal
Daily Readings from Every Day a Friday
Fresh Start
Fresh Start Study Guide
I Declare
I Declare Personal Application Guide
The Power of I Am
The Power of I Am Journal
The Power of I Am Study Guide
Daily Readings from The Power of I Am
Think Better, Live Better
Think Better, Live Better Journal
Think Better, Live Better Study Guide
Wake Up to Hope Devotional
(with Victoria Osteen)
You Can, You Will
You Can, You Will Journal
Daily Readings from You Can, You Will
Your Best Life Now
Daily Readings from Your Best Life Now
Your Best Life Begins Each Morning
Your Best Life Now Study Guide
Your Best Life Now for Moms
Your Best Life Now Journal
Starting Your Best Life Now

DAILY READINGS

FROM

ThinkBetter
LiveBetter

90 Devotions to a Victorious Life

#1 *New York Times* Bestselling Author

Joel Osteen

Faith Words

New York • Boston • Nashville

FaithWords
Hachette Book Group
1290 Avenue of the Americas
New York, NY 10104
faithwords.com
twitter.com/faithwords

First Edition: May 2017

FaithWords is a division of Hachette Book Group, Inc.
The FaithWords name and logo are trademarks of Hachette Book Group, Inc.

The publisher is not responsible for websites (or their content) that are not owned by the publisher.

The Hachette Speakers Bureau provides a wide range of authors for speaking events. To find out more, go to www.hachettespeakersbureau.com or call (866) 376-6591.

Literary development: Lance Wubbels Literary Services, Bloomington, Minnesota.

ISBN: 978-1-4789-4468-3

Printed in the United States of America

10 9 8 7 6 5 4 3 2 1

Contents

Introduction

Your mind has incredible power over your success or failure to become all you were created to be. We all have our own struggles in life, and the first step in overcoming problems is to get rid of negative thoughts. If we can't think positive thoughts, we can't expect to live a positive life, because our thoughts will determine the life we're going to live. When we start thinking positive, faith-filled thoughts, we have the power within that will enable us to go beyond the ordinary into the extraordinary life we were designed to live.

That is why I wrote my book *Think Better, Live Better*. In it I reveal a simple yet life-changing strategy for erasing the thoughts that keep you down and for reprogramming your mind with positive thinking to reach a new level of victory in every area of your life. As a child of the Most High God, you are equipped to handle anything that comes your way. To claim your destiny, you need to start thinking about yourself the way God does and to delete the thoughts that tear down your confidence.

My friend, over the next ninety days, will you take a journey of a lifetime together with me and explore ten powerful keys for your life:

1. Reprogram Your Mind
2. Remove Negative Labels
3. Release the Full You
4. Think Yourself to Victory
5. Pregnant with Possibility
6. The Promise Is in You
7. Ask Big

This collection of ninety daily devotionals contains excerpts from my original book that will help you to train yourself to tune out the negativity and to tune into your calling, so you may begin to live the wonderful plans God has made for you. It offers the same positive, inspiring, and faith-building messages and encouragement of *Think Better, Live Better* in daily doses supplemented by a wealth of supportive scriptures, selected stories, daily prayers, and daily thoughts for contemplation.

I hope my words and the other material in this daily devotional will encourage you in a process of reflection that will enhance your thinking and help you to rise to a new level of living your best.

Daily Readings from Think Better, Live Better is divided into ten sections. Each section covers one of the ten powerful keys to improving your thinking. The goal is for you to take just a brief time each day to read and reflect, to put the events and circumstances in your life in perspective, and to receive a mental, emotional, and spiritual lift.

Each of the daily readings was selected to emphasize the fact that when we think better, we will see breakthroughs on all that is keeping us back from God's abundant life. I've added several other features to help you apply and live out the truth that God wants you to know. Each daily devotional includes:

A suggested Scripture reading: These passages will sometimes relate directly to the point being described or will provide necessary background for accurately understanding the truth for that day. Reading these selected passages will help you fully benefit from this book.

Key verse(s): A biblical verse that specifically expresses the theme of the devotional.

A devotional excerpt from *Think Better, Live Better*: A brief lesson or story that I believe will encourage and uplift you.

Today's Prayer: A daily prayer that can serve as a model to help you express your prayer requests, desires, gratitude, and fresh commitments to God. Feel free to adapt these prayers and make them your own. Have a personal conversation with your heavenly Father.

Today's Thought: These are points meant for you to consider prayerfully after each daily reading. God's Word tells us that our thinking patterns become our acting patterns. The way we talk to ourselves greatly influences our actions. The Today's Thought sections are meant to encourage you to agree with *what God thinks* of you throughout each day.

By reading at a one-a-day pace, you'll be able to go through these ninety readings in three months or so. As you put these ten key principles into action, your mind will be transformed and renewed as you allow God's Word to refresh and to reshape your thinking, speaking, and daily activities.

Your life can be transformed. Let today be the day when the transformation begins!

ThinkBetter LiveBetter

DAILY READINGS
—— FROM ——
ThinkBetter
LiveBetter

Reprogram Your Mind

DAY 1

You Have the Right Software

Scripture Reading: 2 Samuel 9

For as he thinks in his heart, so is he...

PROVERBS 23:7 AMP

Our mind is like a computer. How we program it is the way it's going to function. You can have the most powerful computer ever made, the latest and fastest model, with the maximum amount of memory available, but if you put the wrong software in it, it's not going to function as it was designed. We've all had to deal with computer viruses. They can get into a perfectly good computer and start to contaminate the software. Before long the computer is slow, then you can't access your files. None of these problems occur because it's defective or poorly made. The computer's hardware is fine. It's because somebody reprogrammed the software. Somehow the insides got messed up. Now the software is contaminated.

In a similar way, when God created you, He stepped back and said, "Another masterpiece." Your hardware is perfect. You're the right size, the right nationality, and you have the right gifts. Not only that, God put the right software in you. From the very beginning, He programmed you to be victorious, healthy, strong, and creative. He programmed, "Whatever you touch will prosper and succeed." He programmed, "You are the head and not the tail. You will lend and not borrow. You are a victor and not a victim."

The reason we don't always experience this abundant life is that we've allowed viruses to contaminate our software. We say to ourselves, "I'll never be successful. I'm not that talented."

"I'll never break this addiction. I've had it too long." "I'm slow, clumsy, and unattractive. Nothing good is in my future." Because our software is infected, we go around with low self-esteem, we're negative, we don't believe our dreams will come to pass, and we don't expect problems to turn around.

Here's the good news, though. Like that computer, there is nothing wrong with you. You're not defective or faulty. The problem is in your software. You have to get rid of the viruses. All through the day, dwell on what your Creator says about you. "I'm blessed. I'm strong. I'm healthy. I'm confident. I'm attractive. I'm valuable. I'm victorious." You have to get back to your original software. If your thinking is limited, your life will be limited. When you think better, you'll live better.

Today's Prayer
Father, thank You for creating me with the perfect
hardware. I am the right size, the right nationality, and I
have the right gifts and the right software in me. I declare
that You programmed me to be victorious, healthy,
strong, and creative. In Jesus' Name. Amen.

Today's Thought
You were programmed to live an abundant, victorious,
faith-filled life. Your original software says, "You
can do all things through Christ." That's how
your Creator designed you.

Learn to Hit the Delete Button

Scripture Reading: Psalm 139

*I praise you because I am fearfully and wonderfully made;
your works are wonderful, I know that full well.*

PSALM 139:14

To restore our original software, one of the best things we can learn to do is hit the delete button. When negative, discouraging thoughts come trying to contaminate your software, just hit delete before they start affecting how you live. That thought says, *You've seen your best days. It's all downhill from here.* Recognize that's a virus trying to keep you from your destiny. It's real simple. Delete. Say to yourself, "I'm not dwelling on that. My software says, 'The path of the righteous gets brighter and brighter.'"

You'll never get well. You saw the medical report. Delete. Replace it by saying, "God is restoring health to me. The number of my days He will fulfill."

You'll never accomplish your dreams. You're not that talented. You don't have what it takes. Delete. Delete. Delete. "I am fearfully and wonderfully made. I have the favor of God. Whatever I touch prospers and succeeds."

You'll never break that addiction. Your father was an alcoholic, and you'll be one, too. Delete. "No weapon formed against me will prosper. Whom the Son sets free is free indeed, and I am free."

If you're going to reach your highest potential, you have to get good at hitting the delete button.

When I stepped up to pastor the church, every thought told me, *You can't do this, Joel. You don't know how to minister.*

You're too young. You don't have the experience. Nobody is going to come. It would have been easy to let that virus take root and keep me from my destiny. I did what I'm asking you to do. I kept hitting the delete button. *You can't do it.* Delete. *You're too young.* Delete. *Nobody is going to come.* Delete. *You don't have the experience.* Delete. *It's not going to work out.* Delete. I wouldn't be where I am today if I hadn't become an expert at hitting the delete button.

Today's Prayer

Father in heaven, thank You for giving me the power to delete negative, discouraging thoughts that come to contaminate my thinking. Equip me with the truth and help me to become an expert at hitting the delete button. In Jesus' Name. Amen.

Today's Thought

When negative, discouraging thoughts come trying to contaminate your software, just hit delete before they start affecting how you live. If you're going to reach your highest potential, you will have to get good at hitting the delete button.

DAY 3

Guard Your Mind

Scripture Reading: Philippians 4

*Do not be anxious about anything, but in every situation,
by prayer and petition, with thanksgiving, present your
requests to God. And the peace of God, which transcends
all understanding, will guard your hearts and
your minds in Christ Jesus.*

PHILIPPIANS 4:6–7

The Scripture tells us to guard our mind. You control the doorway to what you allow in. You can dwell on every negative thought and every derogatory comment, or you can choose to delete it and dwell on what God says about you. If you let negative thoughts play over and over in your mind, they will contaminate your confidence, contaminate your self-esteem, and contaminate your future.

Why don't you start hitting the delete button? Quit dwelling on every negative thought that comes to your mind. That's the enemy trying to contaminate your software. If he can control your thinking, he can control your whole life. If the thought is negative, discouraging, pushing you down, don't dwell on it. Delete it. Pay attention to what you're thinking. If you go around thinking that you're not talented, you'll never have the confidence to step into your destiny. If you think you're unattractive, you'll never meet the people you were supposed to meet. If you think you've reached your limits, you have. It's not because you can't go further. You've just convinced yourself that you can't.

The good news is that it's not too late. You can still become everything God created you to be. Here's a key: Clear out the negative things that people have said about you. The coach or the teacher said, "You don't have what it takes." Delete it. Quit dwelling on that. You're the right size. You have exactly what you need for the race that's been designed for you.

Clear out what the counselor said. "You're just a C student. You're not college material." Delete it. You're an A student. You have seeds of greatness.

Clear out what the ex-boyfriend or the ex-spouse said. "You're not attractive. You're not good enough for me." Delete it. You're a masterpiece, one of a kind, beautiful, attractive, a prized possession.

You may have to clear out what a parent said about you. "You're so undisciplined. You're never going to amount to much. You can't do anything right." Delete it. You are destined to do great things. You're destined to leave your mark on this generation.

Today's Prayer

Father, help me to take control of the doorway to my mind and to stop allowing negative thoughts to enter and play over and over. Thank You for Your power that helps me to clear out all the negative thoughts from my mind and dwell on what You have to say about me.
In Jesus' Name. Amen.

Today's Thought

You have to clear out all the negative things that people have said about you. You are not who people say you are. You are who God says you are.

DAY 4

Water the Right Seeds

Scripture Reading: Joshua 1

*"Meditate on [the Word of God] day and night, so that
you may be careful to do everything written in it.
Then you will be prosperous and successful."*

Joshua 1:8

I read a report about children who had been bullied in school.
It talked about how, years later, negative words from bullies,
such as "fat" and "loser" and "failure," were still having an effect
on many of them. They made the mistake of letting those words
take root in their thinking, and it had a dramatic impact on
their lives.

When somebody calls you something, either good or bad,
that seed is planted in your soil. Now you get to determine
whether or not that seed takes root and grows. When you dwell
on what was said, you are watering the seed. You're giving it a
right to become a reality. That's why it's so important that we're
disciplined in our thought life. It's great when people tell you,
"You're blessed. You're talented. You're going to do great things."
Water those seeds. Meditate on those throughout the day. That's
what you want to become a reality.

But too often we make the mistake of watering the wrong
seeds. If you allow negative things that other people say about
you to take root, it's not their fault. They can't make a seed take
root in you. All they can do is sow the seed. You have complete
control over what seeds are going to grow in your own soil. A lot
of times we blame others. "They were talking about me. They
tried to make me look bad. They were criticizing me." Let them

talk all they want. You control your own soil. Don't dwell on the negative. Don't replay what they said over and over. Guard your mind. Those are viruses trying to infiltrate your software.

This is what the Lord told Joshua after Moses had died and he was to lead the Israelites into the Promised Land: "If you will meditate on what God says about you day and night, you will have good success and prosper in everything you do." When your mind is filled with thoughts of faith, thoughts of hope, and thoughts of victory, that's what will become a reality.

Today's Prayer
Father, thank You for Your instruction to meditate on Your Word and fill my mind with thoughts of faith and hope and victory. Thank You for Your equipping power to water the right thoughts and see them take root and guard them from attack. I believe You will bring me to good success and prosper me in everything I do.
In Jesus' Name. Amen.

Today's Thought
Instead of constantly playing negative thoughts and letting them take root, you should go around thinking, *I'm a masterpiece. I'm one of a kind. I'm talented. I've got seeds of greatness.* Meditate on those thoughts throughout the day. That's what you want to become a reality.

Reprogram Your Software

Scripture Reading: Psalm 27

*Although my father and my mother have abandoned me,
yet the LORD will take me up [adopt me as His child].*

PSALM 27:10 AMP

You may have been through unfair situations. People may have spoken things over you that they had no business saying. You could easily go around feeling bad, having low self-esteem, low self-worth. But don't ever let what someone said or what someone did keep you from knowing who you really are. You are a child of the Most High God.

I talked with a man who was raised by a very negative father who always put him down, telling him what he couldn't become. Not surprisingly, this son, when he was in his twenties, couldn't seem to ever get ahead. Life was always a struggle. He had a college degree, but he couldn't get a good job and couldn't keep a steady relationship. He told how his father's words were always playing in the back of his mind: "You'll never be successful. You don't have what it takes." The last words he ever heard his father speak to him were, "Your brother never amounted to anything, and you won't either." For years he went around with a smoldering anger, feeling inferior, with all of that negativity acting like an anchor on his life.

One day this man heard me talk about making sure you don't have wrong mind-sets that are holding you back. He realized that his father's words had become a stronghold in his mind. He started hitting the delete button, reprogramming his software. When he heard, "You don't have what it takes," he hit delete and said, "I'm equipped. I'm empowered. I'm well able." When he heard, "You'll never amount to anything," he hit delete and declared, "I will fulfill my destiny."

Today this gentleman is extremely successful and has a beautiful family. Everything changed when he started to hit the delete button. Maybe you are like him and you didn't receive your earthly father's blessing. The good news is that you have your heavenly Father's blessing. Almighty God is saying to you, "You are My masterpiece. You are one of a kind. You are equipped, strong, talented, and beautiful." That's what should be playing in your mind. No matter who has tried to tell you otherwise, delete the negative and reprogram your software. You have been fearfully and wonderfully made.

Today's Prayer

Heavenly Father, thank You for making me Your child and for giving me Your blessing. Thank You that there are no strongholds in my mind that Your truth cannot tear down and destroy. I declare that I am moving forward and that nothing can hold me back. In Jesus' Name. Amen.

Today's Thought

You are God's most prized possession. You have royal blood flowing through your veins. God has an amazing future in front of you. If you will hit that delete button and get rid of any strongholds, God will take what was meant for your harm and use it to your advantage.

DAY 6

Break the Strongholds in Your Mind

Scripture Reading: Isaiah 43

But now, this is what the LORD says—he who created you, Jacob, he who formed you, Israel: "Do not fear, for I have redeemed you; I have summoned you by name; you are mine."

ISAIAH 43:1

I know a lady who struggled with her self-worth for many years. Growing up, she never felt she was good enough or that she fit in. These insecurities stemmed from being a child born out of wedlock and being labelled, "Illegitimate." That phrase became ingrained in her thinking. Anytime she tried to move forward, these words would come up in her mind once again: "You're a mistake. Nobody wanted you. You're not valuable." She believed the lies, which dramatically affected her personality, her attitude, and even her marriage.

One day she discovered that our worth and value doesn't come from people; it comes from Almighty God. She said, "It was like something exploded on the inside." She decided to start hitting the delete button. When thoughts came saying, *You're not valuable,* instead of dwelling on them and letting them depress her, she reprogrammed her software. "I'm not an accident. God chose me to be here before the foundation of the world. I'm accepted. I'm approved. I'm valuable." Today, now that her thinking is better, she is living a blessed, free, confident life.

Make sure there are no strongholds in your mind that are keeping you back. I've learned that anytime we try to move forward in faith, there will always be people trying to contaminate our software. They may not do it on purpose, but they'll tell you what you can't do and why it's not going to work out. But remember, God didn't put the promise in them. God put the promise in you. Don't let people talk you out of your destiny.

That's why we start off every message by saying, "I am who God says I am." I like to take it one step further. "Not only am I who God says I am, but I can do what God says I can do." That means we know we've been programmed for victory. We've been programmed to reign in life. We've been programmed to overcome obstacles. We will accomplish our dreams. We will meet the right people. We will step into the fullness of our destiny. When you think like that, all the forces of darkness cannot stop you.

Today's Prayer

Father, thank You that I am not an accident or a mistake. Thank You for creating me, for redeeming me, and for calling me by name. I declare that I am Yours, and I believe that You have programmed me for victory and to reign in life on this earth and for all eternity. In Jesus' Name. Amen.

Today's Thought

The real battle is taking place in your mind. If you're defeated in your thoughts, you've already lost. You have to get rid of the viruses if you want to live better. If you will get back to the original software that was installed in you by your Creator, you'll go places that you've never dreamed.

Consider How You Were Programmed

Scripture Reading: Ephesians 1

I pray that your hearts will be flooded with light so that you can understand the confident hope he has given to those he called— his holy people who are his rich and glorious inheritance.

EPHESIANS 1:18 NLT

It's interesting how little children start off so excited about life. They have big dreams. They're going to become a scientist, an astronaut, a singer, a teacher, a ballplayer, even the president. They're not intimidated or insecure. They believe they can do anything. It's because they just came from their Creator. Their thinking has not been contaminated. They can still feel the seeds of greatness. But over time, too often somebody tells them what they *can't* become, what they *can't* do. Little by little their environment starts to squeeze down on them. A coach says, "You're not good enough." Their self-esteem goes down. They see somebody more attractive, who is getting all sorts of attention, and they start to feel inferior. Before long, instead of dreaming big and believing possibility thoughts, they think, *I'll never do anything great. I'm just average.*

When we find ourselves not believing we can rise any higher, we need to ask, "Why do I think this way? Who programmed me to think that I'm average and to give up on my dreams? Who programmed me to think I can't lose this weight or break this addiction? Where did those thoughts come from?" Could it be that you have accepted a wrong mind-set because of the environment you were raised in, from the people you were around? Just because it seems normal to you doesn't necessarily mean that it *is* normal.

Sometimes we've just learned to function in our dysfunction. Maybe everybody you grew up with was negative, but negative is not normal thinking. Just because family members had addictions and bad habits, it's not okay for you to live that way. Those are viruses that have been passed down, that keep infiltrating your thinking and affecting your living. You are not supposed to go through life feeling inferior, held down by low self-esteem, addicted, having only small goals and small dreams. That's not who you are.

The good news is that those are simply wrong mind-sets you've developed. Start reprogramming your mind with excellence, not mediocrity. Program it with abundance, not lack and poverty. Program it with freedom, not addictions. As you get your thinking straightened out, you will live a healthy, abundant, happy, faith-filled life.

Today's Prayer
Father, thank You that You are the light and even now You are flooding my mind with light so that I can understand the confident hope that You have given me. Thank You for helping me to see and to break those wrong mind-sets that are limiting how I live. I declare that I am who You say I am. In Jesus' Name. Amen.

Today's Thought
God created you to live confidently, to be free, to be healthy, positive, and happy. Get it started by reprogramming your thinking.

DAY 8

Strongholds Are Coming Down

Scripture Reading: 2 Corinthians 10

The weapons we fight with are not the weapons of the world. On the contrary, they have divine power to demolish strongholds. We demolish arguments and every pretension that sets itself up against the knowledge of God, and we take captive every thought to make it obedient to Christ.

2 CORINTHIANS 10:4–5

My father grew up in a very poor environment. His parents lost everything during the Great Depression. He had no money, a poor education, and no future to speak of. He had been programmed with poverty, defeat, and mediocrity. He could have thought, *This is my lot in life. We're just poor defeated people.* But at seventeen years old, when he gave his life to Christ, he started reprogramming his thinking. Deep down, something said, "You were made for more than this. You're not supposed to constantly struggle, to barely make it through life." His attitude was, *This may be where I am, but this is not who I am. I may be in defeat, but I am not defeated. I'm a child of the Most High God.*

Day after day, he kept hitting the delete button. A thought told him, *You have no future.* Delete. "God's plans for me are for good, to give me a future and a hope."

You have no money. Delete. "I'm blessed. Whatever I touch prospers."

You didn't even finish school. You'll never get out of here. It's impossible. Delete. Delete. Delete. "God is making a way where I don't see a way. He is opening doors that no man can shut.

He is bringing the right people across my path. I will step into the fullness of my destiny." He reprogrammed his thinking with thoughts of faith, thoughts of hope, and thoughts of victory. As his thinking improved, he rose up out of that poverty and set a new standard for our family.

You may have been raised in a limited environment. All you saw modeled was strife, addictions, conflict, low self-esteem, and mediocrity. Don't let that set the limits for your life. God wants you to go further. It starts by getting rid of viruses. Hit the delete button. A thought tells you, *You've gone as far as you can.* Delete. *You'll never get well.* Delete. *You'll always be addicted.* Delete. *This is as good as it gets.* Delete.

If you will get good at hitting the delete button, you will break out of bondages and step into freedom. You will break out of mediocrity and step up to excellence. Get ready for God to do something new.

Today's Prayer
Father, thank You that the weapons You have given
me have Your divine power to demolish the lies and
arguments that are set up to keep me from knowing and
obeying You. I declare that strongholds are coming
down and that I am stepping into freedom.
In Jesus' Name. Amen.

Today's Thought
This is a new day. Strongholds are coming down. Wrong
mind-sets are being broken. Viruses are being cleared out.
Get ready to see God's goodness in amazing ways.

DAY 9

Clear Out Every Virus

Scripture Reading: Colossians 3

Set your mind and keep focused habitually on the things above [the heavenly things], not on the things that are on the earth.

COLOSSIANS 3:2 AMP

When Carl Lewis was training for the Olympic Games, the experts said no person can jump over thirty feet. Scientists had run their calculations, done all their research. According to their data, no one could ever jump that far. A reporter asked Carl Lewis what he thought about it. He responded, "Yes, I know the experts say it can't be done, but I don't listen to that kind of talk. *Thoughts like that have a way of sinking into your feet.*" He went on later that same year to jump over thirty feet and break the world record.

Are you allowing negative thoughts to sink into your feet, to stifle your potential, to handicap your life's race? Why don't you do what he did? Start hitting the delete button. God has the final say. He wouldn't have put the dream in your heart or given you that promise if He didn't have a way to bring it to pass.

Delete what the naysayers have told you. Delete the discouraging words. Delete the negative reports. You have to get back to your original software. Who told you that you can't be successful? Who told you that you can only make Cs in school? Who told you you're not tall enough, not smart enough, that you've reached your limits? I can assure you those words did not come from your Creator. Those are viruses trying to contaminate your software. Don't let what anyone told you or what anyone modeled for you limit your life. There is nothing wrong with you. Start reprogramming your mind. All through the day, dwell on what your Creator says about you. "I'm blessed. I'm healthy. I'm talented. I'm valuable. My best days are still out in front of me."

If you'll do this, I believe and declare, every virus is being cleared out, even right now. Strongholds are coming down. Wrong mind-sets that have held you back for years will no longer have any effect on you. As Joshua was promised, you will have good success and prosper in everything you do.

Today's Prayer

Father in heaven, thank You that I can set my mind on what is above, on the truths of Your Word that lift me up. Thank You for the dreams and the promises that You have given to me. I believe that You are bringing them to pass even now, because You are God and You are for me. In Jesus' Name. Amen.

Today's Thought

People may have tried to push you down and make you feel insignificant, but that does not change who you are. God has crowned you with His favor. You are the apple of God's eye. You will succeed and prosper in everything you do.

Remove Negative Labels

DAY 1

Think Better Than What Others Say

Scripture Reading: Deuteronomy 28:1–14

The LORD will make you the head, not the tail.
DEUTERONOMY 28:13

As a teenager, Walt Disney was told by a newspaper editor that he wasn't creative, that he didn't have a good imagination. Lucille Ball was told that she didn't have any acting skills, that she should try a different profession. Winston Churchill was not thought of as a good student and twice failed the entrance examination into the Royal Military College Sandhurst. The common denominator in the success of these people is that they chose to remove the negative labels. Because they thought better than what others said, they lived far better than the labels had read.

People constantly put labels on us, telling us what we can and cannot become, what we do or don't have. Many times, these labels are not in agreement with what God says about us; but if we don't know any better, we'll wear them like they're the truth. If we keep them on long enough, they'll become so ingrained in our thinking we'll become what people have said rather than what God has said.

I met a gentleman whose high school counselor labelled him—"below average, barely getting by, not talented"—and told him to focus on the lowest-skilled job he could find. He wore that label year after year, thinking, *I just don't have what it takes.* He got a factory job and stayed at the lowest level for years. One day he applied at another factory that required every applicant to take an IQ test. He took the test and his IQ score was assessed at the genius level. The owner asked him, "What are you doing applying for this low-level position? You scored the highest of anyone in our company's history." That day this man removed a label that had held him back for seventeen years. He eventually started his own company and invented several successful products that are now patented.

Has someone convinced you that you've reached your limit and gone as far as you can go? Or that you've made too many mistakes? "You're all washed up." "You'll never accomplish your dreams." "You don't have the resources." Don't go through life wearing any of those labels.

People don't determine our destiny; God does.

Today's Prayer

Father in heaven, thank You that I do not have to
live according to what others have said I can and cannot
become or accomplish. Thank You that the negative
labels they have placed on me hold no power over
my destiny. I declare that You alone determine
my destiny. In Jesus' Name. Amen.

Today's Thought

As this man did, if you're going to rise to the next level,
you have to remove any negative labels that are holding
you back. To live better, you need to think better.

DAY 2

Labels Are Like Weeds

Scripture Reading: Isaiah 37

Don't be intimidated in any way by your enemies.

PHILIPPIANS 1:28 NLT

When my father went to be with the Lord in 1999, I stepped up to pastor the church. I had never ministered before. One Sunday, after the service, I overheard two ladies talking in the lobby. One said, "Joel's not as good as his father." The other answered back, "Yes, I don't think the church is going to last."

I was already feeling insecure and unqualified, then *boom*, another negative label was stuck on me. "Not good enough. Not up to par. Inferior." That's the way the enemy works. He would love to put labels on you to limit your thinking and keep you from reaching your highest potential. He knows God has amazing things in your future, so he will try to discourage you, intimidate you, and make you feel inferior.

I tried to remove that negative label, but it wasn't easy. Those thoughts played in my mind again and again. "You don't have what it takes. You're not as good as your father." It was like trying to peel off a bumper sticker that has been on a car for a long time. You peel it, and it tears. You have to keep working and working. I fought those thoughts day after day. Finally, I removed that negative label, and I put on a new label: "I can do all things through Christ. I am strong in the Lord. I am anointed."

If I had made the mistake of wearing that negative label, I don't believe I would be where I am today. Wrong labels can keep you from your destiny. You are not who people say you are. You are who God says you are. People will label you "not good enough, too slow, too old, too many mistakes." God labels you "strong, talented, valuable, more than a conqueror." Those are the thoughts that will help you to live better.

Are there labels holding you back today? What a coach said? What a counselor said? Even negative comments spoken by your parents? The only power that a label has over you is the power that you give it. If you remove it, quit thinking about it, quit acting like it's the truth, then that label will have no effect on you.

Today's Prayer

Father, thank You for empowering me to stand on
the truth that You did not make me inferior or not
good enough. Thank You that You have made me to be
strong and that You have given me talents needed to
fulfill my destiny. I believe that You have amazing
things planned for me now and for my future.
In Jesus' Name. Amen.

———

Today's Thought

Words are like seeds. If you dwell on them long enough,
they will take root and you will become what was said.
Don't go the next twenty years allowing negative
comments to hold you back.

The Battle Takes Place in Your Mind

Scripture Reading: Isaiah 62

...you will be called by a new name that the mouth of the LORD will bestow. You will be a crown of splendor in the LORD's hand, a royal diadem in the hand of your God.

ISAIAH 62:2–3

A man told me how he overheard his junior high teacher telling his mother that he was a slow learner. For thirty years he wore that label around and never had a good job, never had any real success. He just floundered through life under the weight of that negative thought. One day I told him, "You have to remove that label. Your teacher may have been sincere, but she didn't know what God put in you. If you're going to become who you were created to be, you have to say, 'No, thanks. I am not wearing that "slow learner" label anymore. I have another label, which is from my Creator, and He says that I have the mind of Christ, I am full of wisdom, and I can fulfill my destiny.'"

Don't let negative labels hold you back.

I talked to a high school student who was about to take her final exams. She asked, "Joel, will you pray that God will help me to make Cs on these tests?"

"Why pray for Cs and not As?" I responded.

"Oh no, Joel!" she exclaimed. "My high school counselor told me I'm just a C student."

She didn't know any better. Somebody stuck a label on her. She was wearing it around as though it was the truth.

The same God who can help you make a C can help you make an A. Why don't you remove that label? The same God who can help you get by in life can help you excel in life. The same God who can give you an apartment can give you a beautiful house.

Do you need to remove any labels? Perhaps it's the label, "divorced"—*I'll never meet anyone new.* Or the label, "overweight"—*I'll never get in shape.* Or the label, "addicted"—*I'll never break these bad habits.*

This is why some people can't break an addiction. They're wearing the label, "addict." The real battle is taking place in your mind. If you think you're an addict, you will live as an addict. You have to change the label. God says you are free. You are clean. You are healthy. You are whole. Don't go the next twenty years wearing the "addict" label. Put on some new labels today.

Today's Prayer

Father, thank You that what You say about me has the power to remove the negative labels that others have stuck on me. Thank You that You even call me by a new name and are making me to be a crown of splendor. I believe that I will win the battle. In Jesus' Name. Amen.

Today's Thought

Whatever label you're wearing, you're going to become what that label says. You're giving that thought the power to shape and control how you live.

Remove Any Label That Holds You Back

Scripture Reading: Isaiah 46

"I am God, and there is no other; I am God, and there is none like me. I make known the end from the beginning, from ancient times, what is still to come. I say, 'My purpose will stand, and I will do all that I please.'"

ISAIAH 46:9–10

Just because somebody spoke a negative label over you doesn't mean it is the truth. My father was told, "You'll never get out of that neighborhood; all the odds are against you." He removed the label. He changed his thinking and totally changed his life. God took him places he never dreamed of going. "You'll never get well; that sickness is terminal." That's what they told my mother. She removed the label. Thirty-six years later, she is still healthy, whole, and strong. You have the power to remove negative labels.

You serve a supernatural God. He can do what medicine cannot do. He is not limited by your education, your background, or the family you come from. He's not shaken by the things people have spoken over you. He's not up in heaven frantically trying to figure out how to get you to your destiny. He knows the end from the beginning. He already has solutions to problems you've not even had yet. He is all-powerful and all-knowing.

People may have tried to push you down with labels, but if you just remove those labels and get in agreement with God, He will lift you up. He will take you where you could not go on your own. You don't have to figure it all out. All God asks of you is to believe Him. When you believe, all things are possible. When you believe, doors will open that may never have opened otherwise. When you believe better, God will take you from the back to the front. Don't let negative labels hold you down.

People will tell you, "You're all washed up. You've made too many mistakes." If you wear that label, it will keep you from the amazing future God has in store for you. God says, "My mercy is bigger than any mistake." God says, "I will still get you to your destiny." God says, "I will give you beauty for ashes. I'll pay you back double for the unfair things that have happened." You wouldn't be alive unless God had another victory in your future.

Today's Prayer
Heavenly Father, thank You that You are my God, and there is no other. Thank You that You are all-powerful and that You are not limited by my background or by statistics, by what medicine can or cannot do. Thank You for knowing the end from the beginning and being in control of all things. I believe that You are taking me to where I could not go on my own. In Jesus' Name. Amen.

Today's Thought
You've been wearing negative labels way too long. Take off the "failure," "guilty," "condemned" labels and put on these new labels: "redeemed," "restored," "forgiven," "bright future," "new beginning." Begin to say what God says about you!

DAY 5

You Have an Amazing Future

Scripture Reading: Deuteronomy 7

*The LORD your God has chosen you out of all
the peoples on the face of the earth to be
his people, his treasured possession.*

DEUTERONOMY 7:6

There was a young lady in the Scripture named Rahab. She was a prostitute. She had made a lot of poor choices in life. I'm sure many people considered her to be a scourge on society. No doubt she wore the labels of "failure, outcast, not valuable, no future." It's easy to think that God surely wouldn't have any different labels for her to wear; she had made too many mistakes. But God never gives up on us.

One day Joshua and the Israelites were about to attack the city of Jericho, where Rahab lived. Joshua sent two men in to spy out the land. Word got to the king that spies had entered the city. Now they were in great danger. Of all the people whom God could have used to protect His people, He chose Rahab. Risking her own life, Rahab took the men into her home and hid them, saving their lives.

The two spies said to Rahab, "We're going to wipe out the whole city, but because you honored God by showing us favor, we will spare you and anyone in this home." When the city of Jericho was conquered, Rahab and her family were the only ones saved. What's interesting is that Rahab went on to marry a Jewish man named Salmon, and they had a son named Boaz. Boaz married Ruth, and they had a son named Obed. Obed married and had a son named Jesse. Jesse married and had a son named David. This means that Rahab, a former prostitute, is in the family line of Jesus Christ.

What am I saying? You are not what people label you. You are what God labels you. People labeled Rahab as an "outcast, failure, not usable." God labeled her as "chosen, restored, valuable, a masterpiece." When that got into her thinking, everything about her life changed for the better. You may have made mistakes, but you need to remove the wrong labels. Quit thinking about what people have said about you. "He'll never amount to much. He's just too far out." "She'll never have a position of influence. I know what she used to do." "He'll never accomplish his dreams. He comes from the wrong family." Don't believe these lies. God has amazing things planned for your future.

Today's Prayer
Father, thank You that You never give up on anyone, including me. Thank You that just as You redeemed and restored Rahab, You have redeemed and are restoring me to be Your treasured possession as well. In Jesus' Name. Amen.

Today's Thought
God loves to take people just like you and pour out His mercy and favor in ways you've never imagined. But it all starts with your thinking. Don't you dare go through life wearing negative labels.

You Are a Masterpiece

Scripture Reading: Ephesians 2

*For we are God's masterpiece. He has created us
anew in Christ Jesus, so we can do the good
things he planned for us long ago.*

EPHESIANS 2:10 NLT

When I was growing up, I was very small. I grew six inches *after* high school. When I played basketball, at one point I was practically a foot shorter than my teammates. Somehow I got the nickname "Peanut." Everywhere I went, that's all I heard. "Hey, Peanut!" "Good morning, Peanut." During basketball games, in front of the whole high school, I heard, "Go, Peanut! Go!" The cheerleaders even had a cheer: "Big G. Little O. Go! Go!" I was the little O. Nobody said it derogatorily. They just said it in fun. But I must admit it didn't help my self-esteem. Every time I heard it, I was reminded of what I was not. "I'm below average. I'm not up to par." I let that label stick, and I became less and less outgoing, quieter, more reserved, all because of a label that I allowed other people to put on me.

One day I did what I'm asking you to do. I pulled off that label. I realized that when God made me, He didn't make a mistake. He made me just as I am on purpose. I may be small, but I know dynamite comes in small packages. In the same way, you are not too tall, too short, too old, or too young. God says you are a masterpiece. Now put your shoulders back, hold your head high, and wear this label proudly: "Child of the Most High God."

One label that far too many people wear is the label "average." They say, "I'm just ordinary." I've had people tell me, "Joel, there's nothing special about me. I'm just one of the six billion people on the earth."

The truth is, there is nothing ordinary about you. You have the fingerprints of God all over you. The Creator of the universe breathed His life into you. He crowned you with His favor. You have royal blood flowing through your veins. You have a destiny to fulfill, something greater than you could ever imagine. But if it's going to happen, if you're going to become all God has created you to be, one of the first things you will have to do is remove the "average" label, peel off the "ordinary" label. Put on these new labels: "Masterpiece," "Valuable," "One of a kind."

Today's Prayer
Father, thank You that because You have made me,
there can be nothing ordinary about me. Thank You that
I am Your child with royal blood flowing in my veins.
I believe and declare that I am Your masterpiece and that
I am a new creation in Christ Jesus, designed by You on
purpose just the way I am. In Jesus' Name. Amen.

Today's Thought
You were never created to live an average life. God has
an assignment for you that nobody else can fulfill.
You are a part of His divine plan. You have something
to offer that nobody else can offer. Declare
"I'm valuable, I'm one of a kind!"

God Looks on the Heart

Scripture Reading: 1 Samuel 16

*"The LORD does not look at the things people look at.
People look at the outward appearance, but the
LORD looks at the heart."*

1 SAMUEL 16:7

When the prophet Samuel came to anoint one of Jesse's sons to be the next king of Israel, Jesse didn't even bother to bring his youngest son, David, in from the fields where he was taking care of the sheep. Jesse thought, *I know it's not David. He's too small, too young, not very talented, and not as smart as his brothers.* David had all these negative labels put on him by his own father.

When Samuel saw Eliab, David's oldest brother, he was very impressed with his outward appearance, but the Lord said, "It's not him." Six more sons of Jesse passed by, and Samuel said, "Not this one. Not this one. Not this one." Samuel finally came to the end of the line and then asked Jesse, "Do you have any other sons? It's none of these."

"Yes," Jesse answered, shaking his head. "My youngest son, David, is out in the shepherds' fields, but I know it's not him."

God doesn't label people the way people do. People usually look on the outside, but God looks on the heart. God knows what you are capable of. God can see the seeds of greatness He has placed in you. It's so easy to let what someone has spoken over us keep us from really believing in ourselves.

David walked in. Samuel took one look at him and said, "He's the one. That's the next king of Israel." Right then and there, David had to make the decision that I'm asking you to make. He had to peel off the negative labels. He had heard them a thousand times: "too young, too small, doesn't have what it takes."

Like David, you have seeds of greatness on the inside. Nobody else has your exact personality, your exact looks. There is something unique about you. You were created to be a history maker. You're not supposed to live and die with nobody even knowing you were here. You were created to leave your mark on this generation.

Today's Prayer

Father in heaven, thank You that You are not limited to seeing me as other people see me. Thank You that You see my heart, and You know the seeds of greatness that You've put in me. I believe that You created me to make a difference in this world and that You have equipped me to fulfill all Your plans for my life. In Jesus' Name. Amen.

Today's Thought

Quit dwelling on what your parent said, what a jealous sister said, what a cranky coworker said, or what a cynical neighbor said. Don't let their label keep you from becoming all that God created you to be.

Giant Killer

Scripture Reading: 1 Samuel 17

*"...no weapon forged against you will prevail,
and you will refute every tongue that accuses you."*

ISAIAH 54:17

What's interesting is that even though David's brothers saw Samuel anoint David as the next king (see yesterday's Scripture reading), they still tried to stick their negative labels on him. Later, when David left the shepherds' fields to visit his brothers out where the army had gathered to fight the Philistines, his oldest brother, Eliab, said, "David, what are you doing out here, and with whom have you left those few sheep you're supposed to be taking care of?" What was Eliab doing? Sticking a label on him: "inferior, not good enough, irresponsible, intimidated."

David could have said, "Yeah, you're right. What was I thinking? I should get back to the sheep." He could have accepted those old labels and let them hold him back, but this time David had a different attitude. He said, "Eliab, what you say about me doesn't change what God said about me. You're still labeling me 'weak, defeated, and inferior.' You don't realize that I've gotten rid of those labels, and the Creator of the universe, the God who breathed life into me, placed new labels on me: 'giant killer, more than a conqueror, destined for greatness, king of Israel.'"

You may have had negative things spoken over you, even by people who should have been encouraging you. I love what Isaiah said: "No weapon formed against you will ever prosper, but every tongue raised in judgment"—that means every negative label—"you will show to be in the wrong." Notice, God is not going to do it. *You* have to show it to be in the wrong. In other words, you have to remove the negative label. Nothing that was spoken over you has to define you, even if it was from people who raised you or grew up in the same home with you. Nothing that's happened in your past has to keep you from your destiny. Even if you've made mistakes or gone through unfair situations, you can show the negative things to be in the wrong by shaking off the self-pity and moving forward with your life.

Today's Prayer
Heavenly Father, thank You that nothing anyone says about me can change what You have said about me. Thank You that I can refute whatever negative words people have said to me or about me and show it all to be wrong by receiving the labels of truth You have given me to put on. I believe that I am a giant killer. In Jesus' Name. Amen.

———

Today's Thought
Will you dare to do what David did and remove the negative labels? You are not who people say you are. You are who God says you are. Remove the old labels. I'll give you new labels to wear: "giant killer," "history maker," "world changer."

The Promise Is in You

Scripture Reading: Hebrews 12

*And let us run with perseverance the race
marked out for us, fixing our eyes on Jesus,
the pioneer and perfecter of faith.*

HEBREWS 12:1–2

Dale Brown, the legendary coach of the LSU basketball team, told me about the time he was speaking to a group of soldiers at a military base in California. When he finished, a young man came up to him who stood nearly seven feet tall and weighed 250 pounds.

"Coach Brown," the young man said, "I want to try out for our basketball team, but I can barely jump. My legs tire out so quickly that I can only play a few minutes."

"How long have you been in the military, son?" Coach Brown asked, gazing up at him.

"I'm not in the military, Coach. My father is. I'm thirteen years old."

Coach Brown took this young man under his wing and sent him his training program to strengthen his legs and increase his endurance. Three months later, he got a letter from the young man saying, "I've done everything you've asked me to do, but my basketball coach just cut me from the team. He told me that I'm too big, too slow, too clumsy, and that I'll never be able to play basketball." Nothing but negative labels were stuck to him.

Coach Brown wrote him back and said in effect, "Son, if you'll just keep working out, keep being your best each day, and keep asking God to help you, He will get you to where you're supposed to be."

That young man, Shaquille O'Neal, decided to remove the negative labels and ended up going to LSU and playing college basketball for Coach Brown, where he broke all the records and became one of the greatest basketball players who ever played the game. I wonder where he would be now if he had believed the negative labels.

Has somebody told you that you can't accomplish your dreams? God didn't put the promise in them. He put the promise in you. Along the way, there will always be negative voices trying to label you, but God would not have given you the dream unless He had already equipped you to fulfill it. You already have what you need. What may seem like a limitation today—too tall, too short—God can use as an asset. God knows what He is doing. He has designed you specifically for the race that you're in.

Today's Prayer

Father, thank You for the promise that You have put into me. Thank You that You have equipped me with everything I need to fulfill my dream and run the race I am in. Thank You that as I keep my eyes fixed on You, the perfecter of my faith, what others say is a limitation in my life is an absolute asset in Your hands. In Jesus' Name. Amen.

Today's Thought

The experts may have told you what you can't do, what you don't have. Here's what I've learned. The experts can be wrong. Experts built the *Titanic*, and it sank. Amateurs built the Ark, and it floated.

You Have a New Name

Scripture Reading: Genesis 35:1–18

*Rachel was about to die, but with her last breath she
named the baby Ben-oni (which means "son of my sorrow").
The baby's father, however, called him Benjamin
(which means "son of my right hand").*

GENESIS 35:18 NLT

In the Scripture, a lady named Rachel died while giving birth
to her son. Right before she died, she named the boy Ben-oni,
which means "son of my sorrow," based on what she had experienced. Now he was going to go through life being called "son
of my sorrow."

Sometimes people will put a negative label on you, not
because of anything you've done, but because of the pain and
heartache they've experienced. Hurting people end up hurting
other people. Bitter people are quick to stick negative labels on
other people.

After Rachel died, her husband, Jacob, came rushing in.
When Jacob heard the name Ben-oni, he said, "No matter what
he's been through in the past, my son will not be called 'son
of sorrow.' His name will be Benjamin, which means 'son of
strength, son of power, son of my right hand.'"

Benjamin grew up to become a great leader. Out of his family lineage came the kings of Israel, one king after another. God
had a great destiny for Benjamin to fulfill, and He knew that if
he went through life wearing that label, "son of my sorrow," he
could never become what he was created to be. God knows how
powerful labels are.

Maybe somebody has tried to label you average, slow learner, not talented, too many mistakes. God is saying the same thing to you that He said to little Benjamin: "I'm placing a new label on you. No more Son of Sorrow. No more Daughter of Broken Dreams. I'm renaming you Son of Strength and Greatness, Daughter of Destiny and Influence." So start going by your new names: Masterpiece, Valuable, One of a Kind, More Than a Conqueror, History Maker. These are the labels we are to be wearing.

People can call you many different things, but you are not what people call you. You are what you answer to. They can call you slow, lazy, too old. That's all right. Just don't answer to it. Answer to "victorious," "talented," "history maker." If you'll do this, I believe and declare, today is going to be a turning point. The bondages from the past are no longer going to have any effect on you.

Today's Prayer

Father in heaven, thank You for the new name that You have given me. Thank You that I can answer to being a masterpiece, to being valuable and one of a kind. I believe that You are helping me to think better and that the bondages of the past are being broken. In Jesus' Name. Amen.

Today's Thought

As you think better, you are going to rise up and become the son of strength, the daughter of influence, the child of victory, the child of blessing, the child of greatness. You will overcome every obstacle, defeat every enemy, and become everything God created you to be.

Release the Full You

DAY 1

Transformed by the Renewing of Our Mind

Scripture Reading: Romans 12

Do not conform to the pattern of this world, but be transformed by the renewing of your mind. Then you will be able to test and approve what God's will is— his good, pleasing and perfect will.

ROMANS 12:2

Inside each of us is a blessed, prosperous, victorious person. This person is free from addictions and bad habits. This person is confident and secure, talented and creative, disciplined and focused. But just because this person is in you doesn't mean he or she is automatically going to come out. This person has to be released.

The apostle Paul gives us the secret: "Be transformed by the renewing of your mind." In the original language, the word *transformed* is *metamorphoo*. It's where we get our word *metamorphose*. We know how caterpillars metamorphose into butterflies. Paul is saying that if you'll get your thoughts going in the right direction and not dwell on "not able to" thoughts, and program your mind with what God says about you, then a transformation will take place. When your thoughts are better, your life will be better.

Think about the caterpillar, the little wormlike larva that starts off as one of the most unattractive insects. It's very plain, nothing really special about it. But God predestined it to go through a transformation. At a certain point, it forms a cocoon, and metamorphosis takes place. It's a process. Little by little it changes. One day it begins to push out of the cocoon. A leg comes out, then a wing. Soon, its head comes out. Before long, it's totally free from the cocoon. It has transformed from being one of the plainest insects into one of the most beautiful, colorful, and graceful—a butterfly. Instead of having to always crawl and squirm around on the ground, it can now fly to wherever it wants to go.

In a similar way, we all start off as worms, so to speak. Our thoughts, without being retrained, naturally gravitate toward the negative. We think, *I can't take that promotion. I'm not qualified.* Or, *I've made too many mistakes. God could never bless me.* You know what those are? Wormy thoughts. But just because we start out that way doesn't mean we're supposed to finish that way. God has predestined us to go through a transformation—from a wormlike larva that crawls and barely gets by to a beautiful butterfly that soars. Here's the key: It's not up to God; it's up to us. The only way to release your butterfly is to get your thinking in line with God's Word.

Today's Prayer

Father, thank You for the transformation that You are working out in my life through the renewing of my mind. Thank You that I can get my thinking in line with Your Word and change my life. I believe that You are recreating me to soar. In Jesus' Name. Amen.

Today's Thought

There is no limit to what God can do in you and through you when you reprogram your thinking and start believing that you're blessed, valuable, one of a kind, and more than a conqueror.

Break Out of Your Cocoon

Scripture Reading: Ephesians 4

…be continually renewed in the spirit of your mind [having a fresh, untarnished mental and spiritual attitude], and put on the new self [the regenerated and renewed nature], created in God's image, [godlike] in the righteousness and holiness of the truth [living in a way that expresses to God your gratitude for your salvation].

Ephesians 4:23–24 amp

In yesterday's reading, we saw that God has predestined us to go through a transformation, a metamorphosis, through the renewing of our mind. What will keep you in your cocoon? *I'll never lose this weight. My business isn't going to get off the ground. I'm not a good parent.* Those thoughts will keep the full you from coming out. You have to realize there is a great parent already in you just waiting to be released. If you're going to see your metamorphosis take place, you have to be convinced that "In me right now is a great parent. I'm going to renew my mind to get this person out." You may be struggling with an addiction, but in you right now is a person who is totally free. You may be down in your finances. Business is slow. But in you right now is a person who lends and does not borrow, who is the head and not the tail.

When thoughts tell you, *You're never going to change. It's never going to get any better*, just tell yourself, "I'm being transformed. My metamorphosis has already begun." That's how you release the full you. I know people who have incredible talent. They have so much to offer, but they've never gone through their transformation. They're allowing the same negative recording to play in their mind all day long. It's time to come out of your cocoon. God is ready to take you to a new level. He's ready to release a new wave of His favor. Now you have to rise up and say, "That's it. I'm done thinking wormy thoughts. It's my time to be transformed. I know I am forgiven. I am redeemed, talented, creative, and disciplined. I am well able."

That's not just being positive; that's renewing your mind. When you do that, I can see part of your wing coming out. I can see your leg breaking through the cocoon. You keep that up and before long you'll release the full you. You'll be transformed into a beautiful butterfly soaring to places you never dreamed possible.

Today's Prayer

Father in heaven, thank You for all the potential that
You have put into me that is just waiting to be released.
Thank You that my mind is continually being renewed by
believing the truths of Your Word. I declare that the full
me is being released by Your grace working in me.
In Jesus' Name. Amen.

———————

Today's Thought

If you will keep renewing your mind, agreeing with
what God says about you, it's just a matter of time
before that person comes out.

Reprogram Your Thinking

Scripture Reading: Proverbs 29

Where there is no vision, the people perish.

Proverbs 29:18 KJV

Robert grew up with a stepfather who always put him down. He was told again and again that he was slow and couldn't do anything right. Robert let those negative thoughts program his thinking and impact his living. He grew up very insecure, intimidated, with no dream for his life, and got a job as an office janitor. One day his mother remarried. This new stepfather was just the opposite. He constantly told Robert what he could become, how talented he was, and how there was a bright future in front of him. This stepfather spoke faith into him, helping to reprogram his thinking. He asked Robert what he wanted to do with his life.

Robert said, "I just want to be a janitor." He'd had years of wormy thoughts put into him. They don't go away overnight.

The stepfather said, "Robert, you have so much more in you. If you'll go to college, I'll pay for every book, every course, every meal, and every degree."

When Robert heard that, something came alive on the inside. Nobody had ever invested in him. He went to college, and in four years he got his bachelor's degree with honors, then he got his master's, then his doctorate. But he wasn't finished. He went to seminary and received another degree. After four degrees, his stepfather said, "I'm done, Robert. You're on your own!" Today Robert is doing great things, living a life of victory, and helping others. But it would have never happened if he had not renewed his mind. He had to get rid of the wrong programming that had been put into him. When he started dwelling on the right thoughts—better thoughts of faith, victory, favor, and "can do"—that's when the transformation took place. He released his butterfly.

Maybe you've had negative things spoken over you just as Robert had. People told you what you can't do, what you're not going to become. Allow me to tell you who you really are. God says you are blessed. You are talented. You are valuable. You are confident. You have been handpicked by the Creator of the universe. Quit dwelling on what people say you are and program your mind with who God says you are.

Today's Prayer
Father, thank You that Your plans for my life are good
and that Your vision for my life is so much greater than
I can ever imagine. Help me to recognize the negative
thoughts I have allowed into my thinking and to
replace them with what and who You say I am.
In Jesus' Name. Amen.

Today's Thought
On the inside of you right now is a victorious,
successful world changer just waiting to break out.
Your butterfly is waiting to soar! I'm asking you to
release the full you. You are destined to leave your
mark on your generation. When you renew
your mind, transformation takes place.

DAY 4

You Have God Almighty's Approval

Scripture Reading: Galatians 1

Am I now trying to win the approval of human beings, or of God? Or am I trying to please people? If I were still trying to please people, I would not be a servant of Christ.

GALATIANS 1:10

When I first started ministering back in 1999, I was so nervous. I didn't think I could do this. Every voice told me, "Joel, you better not try. You're going to make a fool of yourself. You're not going to know what to say. Nobody is going to listen to you." The enemy would have loved to keep me in my cocoon, thinking those wormy thoughts. He doesn't want you or me to break out and soar and live an overcoming life. He wants us to struggle, to be insecure, to be burdened by addictions and bad habits. It all starts in our mind. If he can control our thoughts, he can control our whole life.

I had to do what I'm asking you to do. All through the day I had to say, "I can do all things through Christ. I am strong in the Lord. If God be for me, who dare be against me?" I spoke those words month after month. Little by little, I started breaking out of my cocoon. A wing started to come out. The first couple of years I was so insecure that if I heard one negative comment, I would get discouraged. I would try to change and make sure everybody liked me. But as I continued to renew my mind and improve my thinking, I realized I didn't need people's approval. I have Almighty God's approval.

What was happening? More of my wing was coming out. A little bit of my leg pushed through that cocoon. The truth is, I'm not totally transformed yet, but at least I'm not still in that cocoon. When I compare myself now to where I started back then, in one sense I'm not the same person. I'm not nervous or insecure. I'm confident in who God made me to be. If somebody doesn't like me, it doesn't bother me the least bit. I'm happy. I'm blessed. My life is so much better. That's what it means to be transformed by the renewing of your mind.

Maybe you're not totally out of your cocoon yet either, but don't be discouraged. God is still working on you. Every day that you think the right thoughts, you are breaking out of that cocoon a little bit more. At the right time you're going to emerge completely and take off flying, and God is going to take you places you could never go on your own.

Today's Prayer

Heavenly Father, thank You that You are transforming me step by step and breaking any control the enemy has had in my mind. Thank You that whether or not I have other people's approval, I have Your approval. I believe that by the work of Your Holy Spirit in my life, I am breaking out of my cocoon more and more. In Jesus' Name. Amen.

Today's Thought

Sometimes our own thoughts will try to convince us we don't measure up. Now you have to do your part and get rid of those condemning thoughts. Down deep, start believing that you are redeemed, restored, talented, and valuable.

DAY 5

You Have Everything
You Need

Scripture Reading: Judges 6

The angel of the LORD appeared to him and said,
"Mighty hero, the LORD is with you!... Go with the strength
you have, and rescue Israel from the Midianites.
I am sending you!"

JUDGES 6:12, 14 NLT

There was a man in the Scripture named Gideon. God wanted him to lead the people of Israel against an opposing army. But Gideon was filled with wormy thoughts about himself and what God could do through him. He was stuck in his cocoon.

One day the Angel of the Lord appeared to him and said, "Hello, Gideon, you mighty man of fearless courage." I can imagine Gideon looking around thinking, *Who is He talking to? I am not a mighty man of fearless courage.* Gideon was just the opposite—he was afraid, intimidated, and insecure. But notice that God didn't call him what he was. God called him what he could become. God sees your potential. God knows what you're capable of. You may feel weak, but God calls you strong. You may be intimidated today, but God calls you confident. You may feel "less than," but God calls you well able. If the Angel of the Lord were to appear to you today, He would say the same thing he said to Gideon. "Hello, you mighty man, you mighty woman of fearless courage."

Why don't you get in agreement with God and start believing what He says about you? Gideon answered the Angel, "How am I supposed to save Israel? I come from the poorest family in

all of Manasseh, and I am the least one in my father's house."
Notice his wormy thoughts. A lot of times, like Gideon, we do
the same thing. "I can't do anything great. I'm not that talented.
If only I was a different nationality…If only I had a better personality…If only I hadn't made so many mistakes…" Get rid of
the excuses. You are equipped. You are empowered. You already
have everything you need to fulfill your destiny. It's in you right
now, but you have to do your part to bring it out.

Today's Prayer

Father, thank You that You see my potential and know
what I am capable of. Thank You that You have equipped
and are empowering me to be strong where I feel weak
and "less than." I believe that You are transforming me
into a mighty overcomer by the power of Your Holy Spirit
at work in me. In Jesus' Name. Amen.

Today's Thought

You may think, *I've messed up. I've blown it. I've failed.
I'm all washed up.* Get rid of what somebody has spoken
over you and start renewing your mind. God can still
get you to where He wants you to be. Believe that
you can still release the full you.

See What You Can Become

Scripture Reading: Isaiah 55

*"As the heavens are higher than the earth,
so are my ways higher than your ways and my
thoughts than your thoughts."*

ISAIAH 55:9

I read about a well-known sculptor who lived on an island in the South Pacific. One day as he was walking by a plantation, he saw several big tree trunks that had been cut down. The owner told him, "They're trash. We're just going to haul them away."

"Do you mind if I take one of them?" the sculptor asked.

The owner said, "You want an old piece of useless wood? Go ahead."

The sculptor hauled the large section of tree trunk away and stood it up inside his hut. He began to walk around it, carefully analyzing it, as if trying to release something that was trapped on the inside. Then he started carving away with precision, day after day. Two weeks went by, and he had carved the most majestic looking eagle, with its wings out, head back, soaring through the air. He put it on his front porch.

One day the plantation owner walked by, saw the eagle, and marveled at the detail and how magnificent it was. He said to the man, "I'd like to buy it from you."

The sculptor chuckled and said, "No, sir. It's not for sale."

But the plantation owner was insistent. "Name your price. I'll pay you whatever you want."

The sculptor finally said, "All right. How about five hundred dollars?"

The man paid him. Then, as the owner was walking away, the sculptor said, "Sir, you just bought back the piece of useless wood you gave me several weeks ago."

The next day the sculptor walked by the plantation. There was a sign out front that said, "Tree Trunks for Sale. $500 Each." The owner had learned his lesson.

Here's my point: The sculptor saw something in that discarded tree trunk that other people could not see. He was able to look beyond the rough exterior, beyond the flaws, and saw its potential. He knew what it could become.

It's the same way with our God. Our Creator can see things in you that other people cannot see. He looks beyond the surface, beyond the mistakes you've made, beyond what somebody said about you, and God sees your incredible value.

Today's Prayer

Father in heaven, thank You that You see everything about me. Thank You that You are the divine Sculptor of my life and that You are shaping me according to Your plan for my life. I believe that Your ways and thoughts are higher than mine, and You will do exceedingly more than I could ever imagine. You are shaping me into an eagle who will soar for You. In Jesus' Name. Amen.

Today's Thought

God still sees the eagle in you. God doesn't just see what you are. He sees what you can become. People may have tried to push you down, but God sees you lifting up off the ground. He sees you soaring.

Royalty Is in You

Scripture Reading: 2 Corinthians 3

*And we all, who with unveiled faces contemplate the
Lord's glory, are being transformed into his image
with ever-increasing glory, which comes from
the Lord, who is the Spirit.*

2 CORINTHIANS 3:18

In the Scripture, a man named Jacob had a lot of flaws. He was dishonest. He even tricked his own brother out of his birthright. Jacob didn't look as though he had much of a future, but God doesn't judge the way we judge. God doesn't look on the outside; He looks at the heart. Even when we make mistakes, God doesn't write us off. He always gives us another chance. Why? Because He can see the butterfly in the worm. He can see a champion in a failure. But it's up to us. The only way the transformation will begin is for you to believe that you are forgiven, believe that there is mercy for every mistake, and believe that you are who God says you are.

One time in the Old Testament, an army invaded Jerusalem and killed their king. For the first time, the people of Israel were without a leader. They were discouraged and didn't know what to do. As they sat there thinking that it was over, the prophet Micah rose up and said, "Now why do you cry aloud? Is there no king in you?" (Mic. 4:9 ESV).

I believe God is saying the same thing to each of us: "There's a king in you." You may have made mistakes, but the king is still in you. You may have gone through disappointments. People may have treated you unfairly. You missed good opportunities.

But let these words sink deep down into your spirit. "The king is still in you." "The queen is still in you." I'm not talking to ordinary people. I'm talking to royalty. By faith, I can see kings. I can see queens. I can see your crown of favor. I can see your robe of honor. I'm talking to children of the Most High God. Now you have to start calling out that king, calling out that queen. You have to release what God put on the inside.

"Well, Joel, this is not for me. I've made lots of mistakes. I've lived a rough life." That didn't change what God put in you. You couldn't be any worse than Jacob. He failed again and again, but as you'll see in tomorrow's reading, God's mercy is from everlasting to everlasting. It never runs out. God will never give up on you.

Today's Prayer

Father, thank You that You can see the champion in me
even when I've failed. Thank You that as Your child, You
have made me into royalty and crowned me with favor.
I believe that I am forgiven, that Your mercy and
forgiveness cover my mistakes, and I am becoming
who You say I am. In Jesus' Name. Amen.

Today's Thought

You have royal blood flowing through your veins.
You are wearing a crown of favor. You need to put your
shoulders back, hold your head high, and carry
yourself with confidence.

Created to Soar

Scripture Reading: Genesis 32

*Then the man said, "Your name will no longer be Jacob,
but Israel, because you have struggled with God
and with humans and have overcome."*

GENESIS 32:28

As we saw yesterday, Jacob was a cheater, but God kept working on him, making him and molding him. One day God said, "Jacob, I'm going to change your name." His name literally meant "deceiver." God said, "I don't want you to be called that anymore. You've gone from a worm to a butterfly. Your new name is going to be Israel." Israel means "prince with God." He went from being called a cheater to being called a king. After that, whenever somebody said, "Hello, Israel," they were saying, "Hello, King." They were calling out his seeds of greatness. They were prophesying, reminding him of who he really was. No doubt he started thinking better: *I'm not a deceiver. I'm a prince. I'm a king. I've been chosen by God. I have a destiny to fulfill.* He renewed his mind. That's when the transformation took place, and life suddenly improved greatly for Jacob.

Could it be that the only things holding you back from a better life are your thoughts toward yourself? You're focused on your mistakes, how you blew it, how you didn't measure up. You have to reprogram your thinking. Get rid of the wormy thoughts. All through the day you should say, "I'm redeemed and restored. I am royalty. I am more than a conqueror."

I believe today is going to be the start of a transformation in your life. Some metamorphosis is about to take place. You need to get ready. Talent is going to come out of you that you didn't know you had. Strongholds of inferiority are being broken. You're going to feel a new boldness, a new confidence to step into the fullness of your destiny. Keep thinking better thoughts. If you will start the renewing of your mind, reprogramming it with what God says about you, you're going to release the full you.

I'm calling out the confident you. I'm calling out the successful you, the blessed you, the talented you, the disciplined you, the excellent you. I believe and declare the king in you is coming out. The butterfly in you is coming out. You're not going to stay where you are. You're being transformed. You're going to soar to places that you could never have gone on your own. Receive it by faith!

Today's Prayer
Heavenly Father, thank You that because of what Jesus has done on the cross, I am redeemed and restored, I am royalty and more than a conqueror. Thank You that strongholds are being broken and I am being transformed in the renewing of my mind through Christ. I receive it by faith. In Jesus' Name. Amen.

Today's Thought
You may have one wing out, and that's good. But God doesn't want you to stay in your cocoon. He didn't create you to crawl and squirm. He created you to soar. It's time to get the other wing out.

Think Yourself to Victory

DAY 1

Close the Door to Negative Thoughts

Scripture Reading: Psalm 19

*Whatever is true, whatever is noble, whatever is right,
whatever is pure, whatever is lovely, whatever is
admirable—if anything is excellent or praiseworthy—
think about such things.*

PHILIPPIANS 4:8

Studies show that we talk to ourselves up to thirty thousand times a day. There is always something playing in our minds. The Scripture tells us to meditate on God's promises. The word *meditate* means "to think about over and over." We need to pay attention to what we're meditating on.

Meditating is the same principle as worrying. When you worry, you're just meditating on the wrong thing. You're using your faith in reverse. If you go through the day worried about your finances, worried about your family, and worried about your future, because you're allowing the wrong thoughts to play, it's going to cause you to be anxious, fearful, negative, and discouraged. The whole problem is what you're choosing to meditate on. You control the doorway to your mind. When those negative thoughts come knocking, you don't have to answer the door. You can say, "No, thanks. I'm going to choose to meditate on what God says about me."

Today, there is a lot of doom and gloom. If you watch the news for very long, you can get depressed—the stock market, the economy, the debt crisis. One phrase I observed in several newspapers was "total fear in the marketplace." People are panicked.

Some people go through their entire day thinking about how bad it is, asking themselves, "I wonder if I'm going to make it?" "What if I lose my job?" "What if my retirement funds go down?" If you dwell on these fearful thoughts, you're going to be stressed out. I like to watch the news, but I've learned not to meditate on the negative reports.

Paul tells us to think on things that are wholesome, pure, and of good report. If it's not a good report, don't dwell on it, because it's going to poison your spirit. Instead of replaying the doom and gloom over and over, replay what God says. Yes, the financial situation may be a little shaky, but God says He will supply all your needs. He said He will prosper you even in a time of famine. He said He will open the windows of heaven and pour out blessings that you cannot contain. Go through the day meditating on that!

Today's Prayer

Father, thank You for giving me Your promises to meditate upon. Thank You that Your Word instructs me to think only on things that are true and right, wholesome, pure, and of good report. I declare that my trust is in You alone and not in anything else. In Jesus' Name. Amen.

Today's Thought

Get your mind going in the right direction. After all, the economy is not our source. God is our source. Our trust is not in the stock market or in the economy. Our trust is in the Lord.

Perfect Peace

Scripture Reading: Isaiah 26

*You will keep in perfect peace all who trust in you,
all whose thoughts are fixed on you!*

Isaiah 26:3 nlt

David said in Psalm 20:7, "Some trust in chariots and some in horses, but we trust in the name of the Lord our God." In modern times, it would say, "Some trust in their money. Some trust in their job. Some trust in what the economists say. But our trust is in the God who created it all. He's called Jehovah Jireh, the Lord our Provider." When you meditate on that, you won't have total fear. You'll have total peace. You'll be at total rest. You know God is in control, and He can give you total victory. But it all depends on what's going on in your thought life. You can meditate on the problem or you can meditate on the promises. You can meditate on the news report or you can meditate on God's report. What you allow to play in your mind will determine what kind of life you live. When you think better, you will live better.

God said, "If you will keep your mind fixed on Me, I will keep you in perfect peace." Notice there is a way not only to have peace but to have perfect peace. How? Keep your thoughts fixed on Him. Pay attention to what is playing in your mind. You can't go through the day thinking, *I hope my child straightens up.* Or, *What's going to happen if I get laid off?* Or, *I might not overcome this illness.* When you dwell on thoughts such as these, you're not going to have peace. Meditating on the problem doesn't make it better; it makes it worse.

You have to change what you're dwelling on. All through the day, go around thinking, *God has me in the palm of His hand. All things work together for my good. This problem didn't come to stay, it came to pass. Many are the afflictions of the righteous, but the Lord delivers me out of them all.* That's thinking better. When you meditate on that, you'll have greater peace, greater joy, and greater strength.

Today's Prayer

Father in heaven, thank You that You are Jehovah Jireh, the Lord my Provider. Thank You that I can put my trust in You completely and fix my mind on You. I believe and declare that You give me perfect peace and I will rest in You in all the circumstances of my life. In Jesus' Name. Amen.

Today's Thought

If you don't set your mind, the enemy will set it for you. He will remind you of how bad you have it, how many mistakes you've made, and all the people who have come against you, on and on. Your life is going to follow your thoughts.

Think Yourself Happy

Scripture Reading: Psalm 118

*"I think myself happy, King Agrippa, because today
I shall answer for myself before you concerning
all the things of which I am accused..."*

ACTS 26:2 NKJV

The apostle Paul understood the principle that happiness starts in our thinking. Paul had been through a lot of disappointments and hardships. He had been shipwrecked, put in jail, and mistreated, yet he wasn't focused on his problems. He wasn't meditating on how bad it was, replaying all his disappointments. He's the one who said, "Thanks be to God who always causes me to triumph. I am more than a conqueror." His mind was filled with thoughts of hope, thoughts of faith, thoughts of victory. Paul was saying, "It may look bad, but my mind is filled with thoughts of hope, faith, and victory."

Some people have thought themselves depressed. They have focused on their problems for so long they've thought themselves discouraged. They watched so many news reports they've thought themselves afraid. The good news is that just as you can think yourself depressed and fearful and negative, you can think yourself happy. You can think yourself peaceful. You can even think yourself into a better mood.

The Scripture tells us, "Arise from the depression that has kept you down. Rise to a new life." The first place in which we have to arise is our thinking. You have to put on a new attitude with better thoughts. Don't go through the day thinking about your problems, dwelling on who hurt you. That's going to keep you discouraged. You need to start thinking yourself happy. All through the day we should go around thinking, *My best days are in front of me. Something big is coming my way. What's meant for my harm, God is going to use to my advantage. My greatest victories are still in my future.* Purposefully think power thoughts: *I'm strong. I'm healthy. I'm blessed.* When you wake up in the morning and thoughts come to you saying, *You have so many problems. You have so much coming against you, more than ever,* counter those thoughts by declaring, "This is going to be a great day. This is the day that the Lord has made. I'm excited about my future. Something good is going to happen to me today."

Today's Prayer

Father, thank You that You have made this day, and every day, for me to rise up and be more than a conqueror. Thank You that I can think myself happy by filling my mind with thoughts of hope, faith, and victory as I focus on You and Your promises to me. I declare that my best days are in front of me. In Jesus' Name. Amen.

Today's Thought

Don't start the day in neutral. You cannot wait to see what kind of day it's going to be. You have to *decide* what kind of day it's going to be. When you first get out of bed in the morning, you need to set your mind in the right direction.

You Become What You Believe

Scripture Reading: Matthew 9

*As Jesus left the house, he was followed by two blind
men crying out, "Mercy, Son of David! Mercy on us!"
When Jesus got home, the blind men went in with him.
Jesus said to them, "Do you really believe I can do this?"
They said, "Why, yes, Master!" He touched their
eyes and said, "Become what you believe."
It happened. They saw.*

MATTHEW 9:27–29 MSG

Jesus said to two blind men whom He healed, "Become what you believe." If you believe you'll never meet the right person and get married, unfortunately, you probably won't. Your faith is working. If you believe you'll never get out of debt, you won't. If you believe you're going to get laid off, don't be surprised if you do. You're going to become what you believe. I'm asking you to believe what God says about you. Believe that you are blessed. Believe that your best days are in front of you. Believe that you're strong, healthy, talented, creative, and well able. Get rid of those wrong thoughts that are contaminating your thinking, and start meditating on what God says about you.

The writer of Psalm 1 said, "If you will meditate on God's Word day and night, you will be like a tree planted by the water. Your leaf will not wither, but you will bear fruit in every season without fail." Notice that it is not in *some* seasons but in *every* season of your life. That means even if the economy goes down, you'll still be bearing fruit. It means that when others are going under, you'll be going over. When others have total fear, you'll have total peace. When others are complaining, you'll have a song of praise. When others are surviving, you'll be thriving.

The Message Bible translation of Psalm 1 says that when you meditate on God's Word day and night, "You're a tree…always in blossom." That's God's dream for your life—that you always have a smile, that you're always in peace, that you're always excited about your future. And no, it doesn't mean that you'll never have adversities. But in those difficult times, because you have your thoughts fixed on Him, deep down there will be a confidence, a knowing that everything is going to be all right. You will know that God is still on the throne. He is fighting your battles, and you're not only going to come out, you're going to come out better off than you were before.

Today's Prayer

Heavenly Father, thank You that in every season of my life I can bear fruit like a tree planted by the water. Thank You for giving me Your Word to meditate upon. I declare that I believe what Your Word says, and I am going to become what I believe. In Jesus' Name. Amen.

Today's Thought

Take inventory of what's playing in your mind, and start meditating on what God says about you. The bottom line is that you're going to become what you believe.

Always Be in Blossom

Scripture Reading: Psalm 1

*You thrill to God's Word, you chew on Scripture
day and night. You're a tree replanted in Eden,
bearing fresh fruit every month, never dropping
a leaf, always in blossom.*

PSALM 1:2–3 MSG

I have friends who live in another state. The man works in sales for a large corporation. Recently he got the huge promotion that he had been hoping to receive for a long time. My friends were so excited, but it meant they had to move to a different city. The problem was that the housing market in their area was very down. Hardly anything was selling. They couldn't afford two house payments, so they had to sell their house before he could take the promotion. But instead of getting discouraged and thinking, *Just our luck, got the promotion at the wrong time. Our house is never going to sell*, they kept their minds filled with faith. All through the day they went around saying, "Father, You said Your favor surrounds us like a shield. You said we would always be in blossom. You said You would prosper us even in a famine." That's better thinking.

There were over sixty homes for sale in their neighborhood. In the previous seven months, only three houses had sold. It didn't look good, but they put their house on the market anyway; and two weeks later they had a contract to purchase their home. They talked to the buyers and out of curiosity asked them, "Why did you choose our house?"

The buyers said, "We looked at over thirty houses in the

neighborhood, but when we drove by your house, it just seemed to jump out at us. And when we went inside, we felt such a peace that we knew this was supposed to be our home."

That's what happens when you meditate on God's promises. You will always be in blossom. In other words, your property will sell when others are not selling. You'll get well when the medical report says you won't. You'll be promoted even though you're not the most qualified. Why is that? You have your mind filled with God's Word and know His thoughts toward you. When you're in agreement with God, the Creator of the universe goes to work. God will cause His favor to shine down on you. He will cause your house to stand out in the neighborhood. He will cause you to be at the right place at the right time, making sure that you succeed.

Today's Prayer

Father, thank You that Your plan for my life is that I am always in blossom, that I'm always bearing fresh fruit. Thank You that I can fill my mind with Your Word and know Your thoughts toward me. I declare that I love Your Word. I believe Your favor is shining down upon me. In Jesus' Name. Amen.

———

Today's Thought

Don't go around thinking, *I'm afraid I'm never going to get well.* Your faith is going to draw in the negative. Job said, "The thing I feared came upon me." Just as our faith can work in the right direction, it can work in the wrong direction.

What Is Playing in Your Mind?

Scripture Reading: Job 3

*For the thing I greatly feared has come upon me,
and what I dreaded has happened to me.*

JOB 3:25 NKJV

I heard about a lady who bought a six-foot ficus tree for her bedroom. She loved plants, had them all over her house, and was very experienced at taking care of them. But the next morning, she woke up and thought to herself, *This plant is not going to make it. It's not going to live.* That negative thought came out of the blue, and she made the mistake of dwelling on it, thinking about it over and over. She even told her husband, "I think I've wasted my money on this plant. I'm just afraid it's not going to live."

"What are you talking about?" he asked. "All your plants have lived. Why would you say that?"

"Oh," she said, "something just tells me it's not going to make it."

Three weeks later, for no apparent reason, the leaves on the plant started to turn yellow. A few days later, the leaves had all fallen off. A few weeks later, the plant had totally withered up, completely dead.

One day she was thinking about that dead tree. She sensed God spoke something to her, not out loud but an impression on the inside. He said, "I want you to know you killed that plant with your thoughts."

When she heard that, chills went up and down her spine. When we dwell on the negative, we're releasing our faith in the wrong direction. She told her husband, "I know you're going to think I'm crazy, but I think I killed this plant with my thoughts."

He looked at her very strangely and replied, "All I can say is that I hope you're thinking good thoughts about me."

Pay attention to what's playing in your mind. I'm not saying that every negative thought is going to come to pass; my point is that we can open the door to difficulties by dwelling on the wrong things.

Today's Prayer

Father in heaven, thank You that I can shut the door to difficulties by dwelling on the right thoughts, true thoughts, Your Word. Help me to take inventory of what is playing in my mind. I declare that I will stand against every fear and overcome it. In Jesus' Name. Amen.

Today's Thought

The bottom line is that you're going to become what you believe. Take inventory of what's playing in your mind. The moment you accept that something negative is the norm, it can form a stronghold in your mind that can keep you from your destiny.

DAY 7

Fill Your Mind with the Right Thoughts

Scripture Reading: Psalm 119

Let the message of Christ dwell among you richly as you teach and admonish one another with all wisdom through psalms, hymns, and songs from the Spirit, singing to God with gratitude in your hearts.

Colossians 3:16

I've learned that if you fill your mind with the right thoughts, there won't be any room for the wrong thoughts. When you go around constantly thinking, *I'm strong. I'm healthy. I'm blessed. I have the favor of God*, then when the negative thoughts come knocking, there will be a "No Vacancy" sign. They won't be able to get in.

Once when I was traveling with my father to India, we missed a connecting flight in Europe, and since it was late at night, we went to a hotel at the airport. The young man at the front desk checked the computer and checked it again and said, "Sorry, but we're totally full tonight." When my dad asked to speak to the manager, he even went to his office to do an additional check but finally came back and said, "Sir, I'm so sorry, but I can't make anyone leave the hotel. We have no rooms."

That's how it is when you keep your mind filled with God's Word. A thought of fear or doubt may come knocking, but just like that hotel manager, you declare, "Sorry, fear, there's no vacancy. Sorry, doubt, but you're going to have to go somewhere else to stay."

You need to take inventory of what is occupying the rooms

of your life. If you give fear a room, faith gets left outside. There's not room for both. If you give "I can't" a room, "I can" is left outside. If you give lack, barely get by, "I'll never make it" a room, then increase, promotion, and abundance are left outside. Get rid of the wrong thoughts and let what God says about you have a permanent home.

Think of it like this. Before you go to bed at night, you lock the doors to your house. You don't want any strangers coming in. That's your home. You need to have that same thinking when it comes to your mind. "This is where I live. This is who I am. This is my future. I'm not going to let just any thought come in and have a permanent home. I'm going to guard the doorway to my mind and only give a room to thoughts of hope, thoughts of faith, and thoughts of victory."

Today's Prayer
Father, thank You that I can let the message of Jesus dwell richly in all the rooms of my life. Thank You for all the wisdom, psalms, hymns, and songs of faith that are filling my mind. I declare to every fear and doubt that there is no vacancy. In Jesus' Name. Amen.

Today's Thought
Quit renting out space in your mind to your problems and self-pity. Don't rent it out to can't-do-it, not-going-to-happen thoughts. Serve an eviction notice. Tell those negative thoughts, "You've occupied my rooms long enough. I've got a new resident coming in. My new resident is faith, joy, peace, and healing. My new tenant is victory."

People Do Not Have the Final Say

Scripture Reading: Mark 5

There came some from the ruler's house, who said [to Jairus], Your daughter has died. Why bother and distress the Teacher any further? Overhearing *but ignoring what they said, Jesus said to the ruler of the synagogue, Do not be seized with alarm and struck with fear; only keep on believing.*

MARK 5:35–36 AMPC

When you receive negative reports, I'm not saying to deny the reports that are true and to act as though they don't exist. I'm simply saying: Don't dwell on them. Don't let them consume you to where that's all you think and talk about. Learn to put things in perspective.

In today's Scripture reading, Jesus was on His way to pray for a girl who was very sick, but He kept getting delayed. Finally, people from her house came and said, "Tell Jesus it's too late. She's already dead." Jesus overheard the negative report, but He chose to ignore it. He didn't let it take root. He didn't meditate on it. He didn't get discouraged. He didn't turn around and go back home. He also didn't deny that the report was true or pretend the person had not died.

Jesus knew people don't have the final say. God has the final say. Sometimes in order to stay in faith you have to ignore a negative report. You have to ignore what somebody said about you. You have to ignore what your own thoughts are telling you. You may hear it, but you can do like Jesus and choose not to dwell on it.

In life there will be times when it feels as though every voice is telling you, "You can't do it. It's not going to work out. You'll never overcome this problem." It may be the voices of the people around you, the critics, the naysayers. Or it may just be voices in your mind, thoughts trying to discourage you. You have to choose to ignore it, and choose to believe a better report.

When our children were younger, occasionally one of them would be talking too much, and if the other child didn't want to hear any more, they would put out an arm and say, "Talk to the hand." That meant, "You're talking, but I'm not listening." That's what we need to do when negative thoughts come. In your imagination, just extend your arm and say, "Talk to the hand. I'm not listening to you."

Today's Prayer

Heavenly Father, thank You that no matter what happens in my life, You have the final say. Thank You that I can stay in faith and choose to not dwell on negative reports. I believe that as I get my thoughts in agreement with Your Word that I shall overcome. In Jesus' Name. Amen.

Today's Thought

Don't be surprised if the enemy even starts replaying your failures, replaying the times when you've been too late. If you will get in agreement with God and not let those distractions pull you off course, God will get you to where He wants you to be.

DAY 9

Victory Starts in Your Thinking

Scripture Reading: 2 Corinthians 4

*So we fix our eyes not on what is seen, but on
what is unseen, since what is seen is temporary,
but what is unseen is eternal.*

2 CORINTHIANS 4:18

I was watching an important playoff football game several years ago. There were only a few seconds left on the clock. The visiting team was down by two points, and they were setting up to attempt a field goal to win the game. The kicker was on the field, lining up, getting ready for the biggest kick of his life. The opposing fans were screaming at him so loud, trying to distract him. Just as he was about to kick, the other team called a timeout to give the fans more time to try to intimidate him. On the stadium's big screen, they started playing video clips of the times this kicker had missed in the past. Going back many years, they replayed his failures, and every time he missed, the crowd went crazy. With eighty thousand people screaming against him, he stepped up and kicked the ball right through the uprights and won the game.

Afterward a reporter asked him how he could handle that kind of pressure. He said, "I didn't hear anybody screaming. I just kept telling myself, 'You can do this. You have what it takes.'"

The reporter said, "Well, what about on the big screen when they were replaying all your failures?"

"I saw that," he answered with a smile, "but I just ignored it."

Friend, the first place we lose the victory is in our own thinking. You may feel as though eighty thousand voices are screaming against you right now, saying, "It's never going to work out. This problem is too big. You might as well just settle where you are."

The whole key is what's going on in your thought life. If you'll keep your thoughts fixed on what God says, you will overcome the obstacles and accomplish your dreams. Joshua 1:8 says that if you will meditate on God's Word day and night, you will prosper and have good success.

What are you meditating on? Make a decision that you're going to keep your thoughts fixed on what God says. Purposefully think power thoughts: *I'm strong. I'm talented. I'm creative. I have the favor of God.* Remember, you're going to become what you believe.

Today's Prayer

Father, thank You that I can turn my thoughts away from whatever is opposing me and fix my eyes upon You and what You have promised to me in Your Word. Thank You that what is seen is only temporary, but what is unseen is eternal. I believe that I will accomplish the dreams You have for me. In Jesus' Name. Amen.

Today's Thought

When you get up every morning, set your mind in the right direction. Don't meditate on the problem. Meditate on the promises. Think yourself victorious. Victory starts in your thinking.

Pregnant with Possibility

DAY 1

Live with Expectancy

Scripture Reading: Philippians 1

*...being confident of this, that he who began a
good work in you will carry it on to completion
until the day of Christ Jesus.*

PHILIPPIANS 1:6

When a woman is pregnant, for the first few months she typically doesn't look any different. She's the same size, wears the same clothes, and has the same amount of energy. From the outside, there's no sign that she's going to have a baby. If you just looked at it in the natural, you could think, *She's not pregnant. There's nothing different about her.* But what you can't see is that on the inside a seed has taken root. Conception has occurred. A few months into the pregnancy, she'll start showing, gaining more weight. Weeks later, she'll feel something kicking on the inside. Suddenly a kick here, a kick there. She's still never seen the baby in person. She's never held that baby, but she knows the baby is on the way. Nine months after she conceives, she'll give birth to that little child.

In a similar way, you may not realize it, but you are pregnant. God has placed all kinds of potential in you. There are gifts, talents, and ideas. He's put dreams, businesses, books, songs, healing, and freedom inside you. You are pregnant with possibilities, pregnant with increase, pregnant with healing.

As was true for this woman, you may not see any sign of the pregnancy at the beginning, but don't worry. You are pregnant with your miracle, pregnant with abundance. Maybe you're pregnant with a new business. Instead of being discouraged and thinking, *It's never going to happen. It's been so long. I've been through too much*, your attitude should be, *I can feel something kicking on the inside. I know something good is growing. I'm going to give birth to what God put in me.*

Maybe you've struggled with an addiction for a long time. Instead of believing the lie that says you can never break free, say, "No, I'm pregnant with freedom. I'm pregnant with wholeness. You may not see any changes in me, but I can feel something kicking. I can feel something stirring down in my spirit." When you live with this kind of expectancy, you're going to give birth to what God put in you.

Today's Prayer

Father in heaven, thank You for all the potential You have placed in me, all the gifts, talents, and ideas. Thank You that the seed has taken root in my life and is growing. I fully expect and declare that I will give birth to what You have put in me. In Jesus' Name. Amen.

Today's Thought

Just because you don't see anything happening doesn't mean it's not going to come to pass. The seed God put in you has already taken root. Conception has occurred. Your time is coming.

DAY 2

Give Birth to What God Put in You

Scripture Reading: Luke 18

But He said, "The things which are impossible with men are possible with God."

Luke 18:27 nkjv

Psalm 7:14 says the ungodly "are pregnant with trouble and give birth to lies" (NLT). The good news is: That's not you. You are the righteous. You're not pregnant with trouble, with bad breaks, sickness, lack, or depression. You are pregnant with favor, pregnant with talent, pregnant with victory. All through the day, keep saying, "Lord, thank You that I'm pregnant with Your promises, that I will give birth to everything You've put in me." You may not see any changes. It may not look in the natural as though it's ever going to work out, but deep down in your spirit, you choose to believe that conception has occurred. In God's perfect timing, when everything is ready, you're going to give birth.

Your family may be struggling with dysfunction in your home. Don't live worried. You are pregnant with restoration, pregnant with the breakthrough. Maybe business is slow and you lost your main client. You could easily be discouraged, but you can feel something kicking on the inside, something saying, "You are the head and not the tail. Whatever you touch will prosper and succeed." Perhaps your dream looks impossible. It's been a long time, you gave it your best effort, and it didn't work out; but deep down you can't help it—something keeps kicking, telling you that it's still on the way. What God started, He will finish.

I talked to a gentleman recently who was diagnosed with cancer. The doctors told him it was a very invasive type that would spread quickly to other areas. After the scheduled surgery, he was going to have to take one year of chemotherapy. The prognosis didn't look good, but he didn't get depressed. He didn't go around saying, "Why me, God?" He understood the principle that he was pregnant with healing. The doctors performed the surgery. Afterward they came into his hospital room scratching their heads. They had been certain it was a dangerous invasive type of cancer, but when they had it retested, it wasn't what they had thought. They were able to remove all the cancer, he didn't need any more treatment, and today he's totally cancer-free.

Today's Prayer
Father, thank You that I can put away any worries and discouragements. Thank You that in Your perfect timing, when everything is ready, even what looks to be impossible is possible with You. I believe that what You've started in my life You will finish. I will obey Your Word.
In Jesus' Name. Amen.

———

Today's Thought
Quit telling yourself that you can never get ahead, that you don't have enough of this, enough of that. You are pregnant with success, pregnant with ideas, pregnant with your destiny. You're going to give birth to what God put in you.

DAY 3

Don't Go by Your Circumstances

Scripture Reading: Genesis 17

Abraham fell facedown; he laughed and said to himself,
"Will a son be born to a man a hundred years old?
Will Sarah bear a child at the age of ninety?"

GENESIS 17:17

In the Scripture, Sarah was over ninety years old when she gave birth to Isaac. This is way too old in the natural, but we serve a supernatural God. He can make a way where you don't see a way. Don't talk yourself out of your dreams. Don't give up on what God promised you. You can still give birth. You can still meet the right person, still start your own business, still go to college, still break the addiction. That seed is alive in you.

Here's the key: You can't judge what's in you by what's around you. All of Sarah's circumstances said, "You'll be barren your whole life. You're too old. No woman your age has babies. It's impossible." If she had believed that lie and let that seed take root, the miracle birth would never have happened. You can draw in the negative with your doubt or you can draw in God's blessings with your faith. Don't let what you see around you cause you to give up on your dreams.

I was in a large city recently. Part of the city was very beautiful, but another part was very run-down, with miles and miles of abandoned homes. When we drove through one neighborhood, there were hundreds, if not thousands, of people outside—young and old, just hanging out, with no apparent purpose, no direction. For most of these people, that's all they've ever known.

They were born into it. They grew up in the projects, living in the midst of drugs, dysfunction, and violence.

You may be in some kind of limited environment today. In the natural, there's no obvious way that you can get out, get an education, and become successful, but what's around you does not determine what God put in you. You have seeds of greatness. You are pregnant with success, pregnant with ability, pregnant with talent. God did not create anyone in whom He did not put something significant on the inside. Don't let what's on the outside—how you were raised, the lack, the dysfunction—convince you to abort your dream. You're going to see supernatural opportunities, explosive blessings, and divine connections. God is going to help you go where you could not go on your own.

Today's Prayer

Heavenly Father, thank You that I am not limited by my circumstances. Thank You that what surrounds me does not determine the seeds of greatness that You have placed within me. I believe that the amazing supernatural plans You have for me are going to take me where I could never go on my own. In Jesus' Name. Amen.

Today's Thought

When you get quiet, alone at night, when it's just you and God, if you listen carefully, you'll hear someone whispering, "This is not your destiny. You were made for more." What is that? That's your baby kicking. It's because you're going to give birth.

It's Just a Matter of Time

Scripture Reading: Psalm 65

You crown the year with a bountiful harvest; even the hard pathways overflow with abundance.

PSALM 65:11 NLT

This is what happened to my father. Statistics during the Great Depression said he would have to stay on the farm and pick cotton the rest of his life. Nobody in his family had done anything different. But statistics don't determine your destiny; God does. Don't become a victim of your environment. Where you are is not who you are.

Daddy told me, "Joel, when I was seventeen years old, I made the decision that my children would never be raised in the poverty and lack that I was raised in." What happened? He became pregnant. He could feel that baby kicking on the inside. But if someone were to have studied my father in that limited environment, they would've said, "John, there's nothing special about you. You're not going to do anything great." In other words, "You're not pregnant. There's no sign on the outside. You're not showing. You look just the same." But what they couldn't see was that conception had already occurred. My father looked the same on the outside, but on the inside a seed had taken root. He knew he was destined to leave his mark on his generation. He didn't let people talk him out of it. He didn't let his environment hold him back. He had better thoughts. He kept praying, believing, and taking steps of faith. He gave birth to everything God put in him.

As was true for my father, the odds may be stacked against

you. You may be fighting a battle in your health. The medical report doesn't look good or your environment is not healthy. Nobody's supporting you, and you don't have the connections or the resources to get yourself there. Don't talk yourself out of it. Keep reminding yourself that you are pregnant. The seed put in you by your Creator has already taken root. It doesn't have anything to do with what you have or don't have, what family you come from, or how talented you are. It is a destiny seed. When you give birth, you're going to go further than you ever imagined.

Today's Prayer

Father, thank You that I can always continue to have better thoughts. Thank You that I can keep praying, believing, and taking steps of faith. I declare that the destiny seed You have placed inside me has taken root and as I walk with You in faith, You will take me further than I ever imagined. In Jesus' Name. Amen.

Today's Thought

Rather than thinking that your life is always going to be the way it is, keep reminding yourself that you are pregnant. You've already conceived. It's just a matter of time before you give birth. Nothing can snatch you out of God's hands.

You Can Be the Barrier Breaker

Scripture Reading: Judges 4

"As for Sarai your wife, you are no longer to call her Sarai; her name will be Sarah…. I will bless her so that she will be the mother of nations; kings of peoples will come from her."

GENESIS 17:15–16

Sarah was eighty years old and had never had a baby when God told Abraham he would have a son as an heir. Everywhere she looked it said that she would be barren her whole life. She couldn't find another eighty-year-old woman who had ever had a baby. If she could have found at least one, she could've said, "God, You did it for her. You can do it for me." But she couldn't find anyone.

You may look around and think, *I don't know anyone who's gotten out of my neighborhood and done something significant. I don't know anyone who's overcome the illness I'm dealing with. Nobody in my family has been able to break these addictions.* The good news is you can be the first. You can set the new standard. You can be the barrier breaker.

God said in effect to Sarah, "I will give you a son. You will be the mother of nations. Kings of people will come out of you." Here's an eighty-year-old woman who's barren. She's living in the desert, with no medical procedures and no infertility treatments available, yet God says, "You have kings in you. You have nations in you." He was saying, "Sarah, don't let the circumstances fool you. Don't let your environment talk you out of it.

Don't let your own thoughts discourage you. You are pregnant with greatness."

God is saying the same thing to you. "You have kings in you. You have greatness in you. You are pregnant with success. Pregnant with talent."

Don't go around negative and complaining. Turn it around with better thoughts. "All my circumstances say that I'll be barren my whole life, never meet the right person, never break the addiction, but deep down I can feel something stirring in my spirit." Or, "The medical report doesn't look good, but I can feel healing kicking on the inside of me. No weapon formed against me will prosper." Or, "It doesn't look as though I can ever get out of debt, but I can feel abundance kicking on the inside. I will lend and not borrow."

Today's Prayer

Father in heaven, thank You for the stirring I feel in my spirit. Thank You that Your Holy Spirit is encouraging me to believe Your promises that speak to the breaking down of barriers that are formed against me. I believe that You did it for Sarah, and You will do it for me as well. In Jesus' Name. Amen.

Today's Thought

Realize that you are pregnant with possibility. It's not too late. You haven't missed your chance. You are pregnant with your destiny.

DAY 6

Wake Up!

Scripture Reading: Judges 5

"Wake up, wake up, Deborah! Wake up,
wake up, break out in song! Arise, Barak!
Take captive your captives…"

JUDGES 5:12

The prophet Joel said, "Wake up the mighty men, wake up the mighty women!" I'm here to wake up your dreams, wake up your talents, wake up your potential, wake up what God put in you. You may have let some circumstances convince you that it's never going to happen, but I believe you're going to start feeling some kicking on the inside. That baby, that dream, that promise is still alive in you. You better get ready. You're going to give birth to something that's going to take you further than you could ever imagine. It's going to thrust you to a new level of your destiny.

A lady told me how she had had a stroke. She'd been in a hospital for three weeks and finally was able to go back home, but she was very depressed. She didn't think she'd ever be able to walk again. She lost her passion, lost her drive. But the Scripture talks about fighting the good fight of faith. You can't be passive and just accept whatever comes along and think that's your lot in life. We all have bad breaks and disappointments. Those challenges are not there to defeat you; they're there to promote you. On the other side is a new level of God's goodness. But you have to do your part and get your fire back.

One Sunday this lady heard me on television talking about how God wants to restore what's been stolen, how He can give you beauty for ashes, how you can still live healthy and whole. Those are better thoughts. When she heard that, she said, something woke up in her spirit. Something came alive on the inside. What happened? That baby started kicking. She was already pregnant with healing. God already had the restoration there, but when her spirit came alive, when she started believing, that's when things began to change. Instead of going around thinking, *I'll never walk again. I'll never get well,* she started declaring, "I am healthy. I am strong. I am well able. I am restored." Against all the odds, she started walking again. She's getting stronger and healthier. It all started when something woke up in her spirit.

Today's Prayer

Father, thank You for calling me to wake up to the promise and the dream that You put in me. Thank You that the challenges of my life, the bad breaks and disappointments, are there to promote me and not to defeat me, to focus my mind on You and Your promises and not my circumstances. I will fight the good fight of faith. In Jesus' Name. Amen.

———

Today's Thought

Maybe, like her, you've let something steal your passion. Recognize that everything you need is already in you. If you'll stir your faith up as she did and get in agreement with God, you will give birth to your healing, birth to your dreams, birth to those promises.

DAY 7

Recognize the True Labor Pains

Scripture Reading: Romans 5

Not only so, but we also glory in our sufferings,
because we know that suffering produces perseverance;
perseverance, character; and character, hope.

ROMANS 5:3

"Well, Joel, I have big dreams, and I'm standing on God's promises, but everything is coming against me. It seems as though the more I pray, the worse it gets. I'm doing the right thing, but the wrong thing is happening." Here's the beauty: Pain is a sign that you're about to give birth. Trouble, difficulties, being uncomfortable—those are signs that you're getting closer.

When Victoria was pregnant with our two children, the first couple of months were no big deal, everything was fine. But about seven or eight months in, her back began hurting, her feet started swelling, and she couldn't sleep well at night. The longer she was pregnant, the more uncomfortable she became. When she went into labor, I was in the delivery room right next to her bed, and she had her hand on my bicep. When she had a contraction, it would hurt so badly she would squeeze my arm as hard as she could. She would scream, then I would scream. The closer she got to the birth, the more painful it was. When everything comes against you—your child's acting up, trouble at work, setbacks in your finances—don't get discouraged. You're about to give birth. You're about to see a promise come to pass.

It is during the tough times that many people abort their dreams, thinking, *I knew it wouldn't work out. The bank turned me down. The medical report wasn't good. I didn't get the promotion.* Recognize that those are labor pains. You're getting closer. Stay in faith. Keep doing the right thing. The birth is on the way. Sure, you may have had some bad breaks, but God has the final say, and He says a birth is coming; what He's promised is on the way. Keep honoring Him, keep being your best, and I believe and declare you will give birth to everything God put in you and become everything God created you to be.

Today's Prayer

Heavenly Father, thank You that anything that is coming against me, any pain and suffering, is only a sign that I am about to give birth. Thank You that I can persevere through the labor pains and that what You've promised is on the way. I will keep honoring You and being my best. In Jesus' Name. Amen.

Today's Thought

Get your hopes up. Every morning, remind yourself that you are pregnant—and not with rejection, failure, disappointments, and defeat. You are pregnant with victory, pregnant with success, pregnant with the favor of God.

Difficulty Is Part of the Birthing Process

Scripture Reading: James 1

Consider it pure joy, my brothers and sisters, whenever you face trials of many kinds, because you know that the testing of your faith produces perseverance. Let perseverance finish its work so that you may be mature and complete, not lacking anything.

JAMES 1:2–3

I heard a story about a young couple out hiking through the woods who came upon a large patch of wild mushrooms. They decided to take some home and cook them. They had friends over for dinner that night. One of the side dishes was the sautéed mushrooms. At one point the large family cat, which loved to eat, came into the room. The husband grabbed some mushrooms and fed them to the cat, which ate them as though they were dessert. About an hour later, he heard the cat making a strange sound. He ran into the other room to check on her; she was lying flat on her back, foaming at the mouth, in intense pain. He called the veterinarian, who asked, "What has the cat eaten recently?"

"Wild mushrooms," the man said, feeling a bit of panic, "but we've all eaten them, too."

"They may be poisonous," the vet stated. "You'd better go to the emergency room and get checked out immediately."

The man and all his guests rushed to the emergency room. A few hours later, when they arrived back at the house, the man went in to check on the cat, thinking that she would be knocked out. Instead, the cat was lying calmly on her side with the seven kittens she had just birthed.

Sometimes what we think is a setback is really just labor pains. That difficulty you're facing is not the end; it's a part of the birthing process. You're about to step into a new level of your destiny. Don't be discouraged by the disappointment, the closed door, or the bad break. That's a sign you're about to give birth to something greater.

Genesis 3:15 says, "The seed of the woman will bruise the head of the serpent." You remember how the serpent deceived Eve in the Garden of Eden and brought about all kinds of trouble. God was saying in effect, "Eve, it's payback time. Despite the labor pains, you're going to give birth to something that's going to defeat the thing that's tried to defeat you. Your seed will bruise his head."

Today's Prayer

Father, thank You that the trials I am facing are not
setbacks; rather, they're just a part of the birthing process.
Thank You that I can face them with a joyful attitude,
knowing that You are going to finish Your work in me
and bring me to maturity and completion.
In Jesus' Name. Amen.

Today's Thought

Jesus said, "Out of your belly will flow rivers of living
water." Give birth to what God put in you. If you'll
go through those labor pains and give birth to that dream,
that gift, that talent, then your promotion, your healing,
your breakthrough is going to come from within you.

Keep Trying, Keep Believing

Scripture Reading: 1 Peter 5

*Humble yourselves, therefore, under God's
mighty hand, that he may lift you up in due
time. Cast all your anxiety on him
because he cares for you.*

I PETER 5:6–7

I read about a man who'd had a rough life. At the age of two, his father left his mother to raise him and a sibling on her own. In college, he met and fell in love with his wife, but he was so poor he had to borrow a suit and tie for his wedding. He and his wife had a newborn baby, and they were living in an old, run-down trailer. He drove a rusted-out car that was held together with wire and duct tape. During the day he worked for a laundry company, and at night he cleaned offices. He had a dream to become a writer, but he couldn't afford a typewriter. He had to use his wife's portable typewriter from college and set it up in their small laundry room.

When this man wasn't working, he spent hour after hour writing fiction stories. He sent manuscripts of his novels to different publishers and agents, but every one of them was rejected. He didn't even know if people were actually reading them. He began writing one final story, but he was so discouraged that he threw the manuscript in the trash. His wife found it crumpled up in the garbage, took it out, and eventually they sent that story to a different publisher. This time the publisher responded and offered him a contract. That story went on to sell over five million books. In 1976, it was made into a movie and became one of the top-grossing films of the year. That young man was Stephen King, one of the most successful writers of our day.

Like him, some of you may be pregnant with a book, a business, or a charity. You've had disappointments—you tried and it didn't work out—but you can still feel the kicking on the inside. You can't get away from it. Don't talk yourself out of it. It's all a part of the process. Keep trying, keep believing, keep doing everything you can, and at the right time you will give birth. The right people, the right opportunities, and the right breaks will show up. You can't make it happen on your own; it will be the hand of God.

Today's Prayer

Father in heaven, thank You that I can humble myself under Your mighty hand, knowing that although I can't make things happen on my own, You can and will. I believe that at the right time, the right people, the right opportunities, and the right breaks will come. In Jesus' Name. Amen.

Today's Thought

What God has put in you is going to be bigger than you could have imagined, better than anything you've ever dreamed, and more rewarding than you ever thought possible. Be patient, persevere, prepare to birth God's destiny for you that will mature, be complete, and lack nothing.

The Promise Is in You

There's Something Special about You

Scripture Reading: Jeremiah 1

*"Before I formed you in the womb I knew you,
before you were born I set you apart..."*

JEREMIAH 1:5

So often, we look at others and think, *Wow, they are so amazing, and I am so ordinary.* Or we'll say, "My cousin is so beautiful, but I'm so plain." We come home from the office and tell our spouse, "My coworker is so smart, and I'm so average." While it's true that they may be amazing in certain areas, you have to realize there's something amazing about you as well. You are talented, you are attractive, and you have been fearfully and wonderfully made. God doesn't want us to go around just celebrating others, cheering them on, although that's good. God wants you to be celebrated as well. You didn't get left out when God was handing out the gifts, the talents, or the looks. He put something in you that will cause you to shine. You can be a great businessperson, a great entrepreneur, a great teacher, a great mother. Don't get so focused on what somebody else has that you don't realize what you have.

During World War II, the famous actress Betty Grable was known for her beautiful legs. Her studio had them insured with Lloyd's of London for $1 million. That was unheard-of back then—a pair of legs worth a million dollars. Do you want to see another pair of million-dollar legs? Look down at your own. If somebody offered you a million dollars to buy your legs, you wouldn't take it.

A few years ago, a man lost his arm in an accident. The court awarded him $11 million for that arm. Look at your arm. It's worth $11 million. In another city, a young lady injured her back while riding in a city bus and lost her ability to work. The city awarded her $20 million. Think about it. Just those three things and you're already worth $32 million. You're starting to feel better about yourself, aren't you? Sometimes we're always celebrating others, but God is saying that it's time to celebrate yourself. There's something special about you.

Today's Prayer
Father, thank You for the amazing people that You've
brought into my life, and thank You that You have made
me amazing as well. Thank You that You formed me
before I was born and gave me the gifts and talents
I have. I celebrate the person You have made me.
I believe that I am fearfully and wonderfully made
in Your image. In Jesus' Name. Amen.

Today's Thought
You have to know who you are. God breathed His
life into you. You are not average. You are not ordinary.
You are His masterpiece. Don't compare yourself.
Celebrate yourself.

It's Time to Step Up

Scripture Reading: Psalm 149

For the LORD takes delight in his people;
he crowns the humble with victory.

PSALM 149:4

For many years, I cheered my father on. Daddy was my hero. When I was a little boy, we used to travel to different cities, and I'd see my father up on the platform, speaking to thousands of people. He was so warm and friendly. Everybody loved him. I was so proud that he was my father. In the back of my mind, I thought, *I could never do that. He's so gifted. He's so talented.* After I came back from college, I worked for seventeen years behind the scenes at the church with my parents, doing the television production. Week after week, I'd watch my father on the platform, ministering, making a difference, doing something great. I did my best to make my father look good. I made sure the camera angles were just right and the lighting was just perfect. I would even go over to his house on Saturday night and pick out a suit and tie for him to wear the next morning for television at the church services.

As my father got older, people would ask, "Joel, what's going to happen when your dad goes to be with the Lord? Who's going to pastor the church?" My father had never designated or trained a successor. Over the years, he tried many times to get me to minister, but I didn't think that was in me. However, when he died in 1999, all of a sudden I had a strong desire to step up and pastor the church. I'd never ministered or been to seminary. Yet deep down, I heard a still small voice saying,

"Joel, you've spent your whole life celebrating others. Now it's time for you to be celebrated. It's time for you to step up to a new level of your destiny." I always knew that God would take care of the church after my dad was gone, but I never dreamed it would be through me. I thought the promise would happen some other way, but I discovered the promise was in me.

God is saying the same thing to you. You've celebrated others. Now it's time to celebrate yourself. It's time for you to think better thoughts about yourself. It's time for you to shine.

Today's Prayer

Heavenly Father, thank You that You take delight in
Your people, and You take delight in me and crown me
with victory. Thank You that You can shine Your light
through me in ways I never imagined were possible.
I believe that You've put a promise inside me
to fulfill. In Jesus' Name. Amen.

Today's Thought

There is a seed on the inside just waiting to flourish.
You may not feel as though you can do it, but God
would not have given you the opportunity unless
He had already equipped and empowered you.
You have everything you need.

What Has God Put in You?

Scripture Reading: Psalm 23

The LORD is my shepherd; I have all that I need.

PSALM 23:1 NLT

I heard about a minister who, before a morning service, handed a man a hundred-dollar bill and asked him to place it secretly in his wife's Bible and make sure she didn't see it. They were all friends, so the man went along with it.

During the sermon, the minister asked this man's wife to stand up. He said to her, "Do you trust me?"

She smiled and said, somewhat hesitantly, "Yes...I do."

"Will you do what I ask?"

She continued her quizzical look and nodded, then said, "Yes, I will."

"Then open your Bible and give me a hundred-dollar bill."

"Oh, I'm so sorry," she offered with a shake of her head. "I don't have a hundred-dollar bill."

"Do you trust me?" the minister pressed a bit more.

"Yes, I do."

"Will you do what I ask?"

"Yes, I will."

"Then open your Bible and hand me a hundred-dollar bill."

Reluctantly, she opened her Bible, and much to her surprise, she saw the money. She shook her head again, laughing out loud, and asked, "How did it get there?"

The minister smiled and said, "I put it in there."

In the same way, God will never ask you for something without first putting it in you. When God gives you a dream, when you have a desire and you know you're supposed to take a step of faith, you may feel completely unqualified. You may tell yourself that you don't have the wisdom, the know-how, or the ability to take the step. But if you'll dare to take that step, just as I did with the church, you'll discover things in you that you never knew you had. I never knew the gift to minister was in me. I never knew that I could get up in front of people and minister to them. I wonder how many gifts are in you right now just waiting to be released.

Today's Prayer

Father, thank You that You are my Shepherd and that in You I shall never want for anything. Thank You for providing me with the gifts, the wisdom, and the know-how to fulfill the dream that You have put in my heart. I look forward to taking new steps of faith and discovering all that You have for me. In Jesus' Name. Amen.

Today's Thought

You may think it's been too long. You're too old. You've missed too many opportunities. God is saying, "You can still do something great." The Scripture tells us to fan the flame, to stir up the gifts, for the promise is in you.

The Promise Comes through You

Scripture Reading: Genesis 21

*Now the L*ORD *was gracious to Sarah as he had said,
and the L*ORD *did for Sarah what he had promised. Sarah
became pregnant and bore a son to Abraham in his old age,
at the very time God had promised him.*

GENESIS 21:1–2

When it comes to receiving God's promise, Sarah, Abraham's wife, almost missed it. She thought the promise from God would come through somebody else. God told her that she was going to do something great. She was going to have a child at an old age and her husband would become the father of many nations. She said, "God, that's impossible. I'm eighty years old. That's never happened. I must not be hearing You right." Thinking it couldn't happen through her, Sarah took matters into her own hands. She had Abraham sleep with one of her maids, Hagar, and they had a son named Ishmael. Sarah looked and said, "There he is, the child of promise."

God replied, "No, Sarah, I didn't say the promise was in somebody else. I said the promise is in you. You spent your whole life celebrating others, but now it's time for you to be celebrated. You're going to give birth. You're going to have that baby. You're going to be a history maker." Those were the better thoughts she should have believed in the first place, which would have helped them avoid so many family problems with Ishmael. Sure enough, when Sarah was over ninety years old, just as God had said, she gave birth to that baby. The promise was fulfilled.

What God has placed in your heart is not going to come to pass through your neighbor, your cousin, your coworker, your friend, or your parents. God is saying, "I've anointed you. I've equipped you. I've breathed My life into you." Now quit looking for somebody else. Quit thinking that you don't have what it takes. You've been chosen by the Creator of the universe. You don't need anyone else to give birth to the promise that God put in your heart.

Today's Prayer

Father in heaven, thank You for the promise that You put in my heart, and I recognize that You are going to bring it to pass through me and not through someone else. Thank You for entrusting it to me and equipping me. I believe that the promise will be fulfilled as I walk with You in faith. In Jesus' Name. Amen.

———

Today's Thought

Instead of responding at first like Sarah, "Okay, God, let me go find somebody younger, somebody smarter, more educated, and more talented," say, "I have what it takes. I won't miss my opportunity. This is my promise—my time!"

DAY 5

You Are the Right Person

Scripture Reading: Exodus 3

*But Moses said to God, "Who am I that I should go to
Pharaoh and bring the Israelites out of Egypt?"*

EXODUS 3:11

D r. Todd Price grew up very poor in a small town. It didn't
look as though he had much of a future. But from the time
he was a little boy, he had a desire to help children in need. One
day he saw a program on television describing how someone
could sponsor a needy child in a third-world country for fifteen
dollars a month. He didn't have any money, but his heart was so
moved that he started mowing lawns to raise the money. When
he was just twelve years old, he started sponsoring a little girl
who lived halfway around the world. What caused him to do
that? It was the promise God put in him. It was a seed of greatness just waiting to be developed.

Dr. Price wasn't raised in a religious home, but every night
before he went to bed, he'd say, "God, please send some wealthy
person to help these children in need." He was able to go to
college, and during the summers, he took trips overseas with a
group of doctors to treat needy children and would pray even
more earnestly, "God, please send some wealthy person to help
these children." He was able to find a way to go to medical
school, and he continued going overseas. Eventually, he started
his own medical practice. One of his main suppliers heard that
he helped needy children and asked if he could use free medical
supplies. Of course he could, and soon a couple suitcases full of
medicines grew to where he had to put the medical supplies in

boxes and have them shipped. Eventually, it expanded so abundantly that he was shipping huge containers of medicines overseas. All the while, he kept praying, "God, please send some wealthy person to help these children in need."

In the last few years, Dr. Price's medical missions organization, International Medical Outreach, has treated over fifty million children in twenty-one countries. He has provided nearly a billion dollars' worth of medicines and supplies. He said, "I finally realized that God had answered my prayers. But it wasn't like I thought. I always prayed for God to send some wealthy person. Now I realize I am that wealthy person." He was saying, "The promise is in me."

Today's Prayer

Father, thank You for the seed of greatness that You are developing in my life. Thank You for your patience with me just as You were patient with Moses. I believe and declare that I am the right person to do all of what You have given me to do. In Jesus' Name. Amen.

Today's Thought

You don't need anyone else to give birth to what God has placed in your heart. Maybe you're waiting for the *right* person. God is saying, "You are the right person. My anointing is on your life. My favor is on your life. You're equipped and empowered. You can do something great."

DAY 6

God Doesn't Change His Mind

Scripture Reading: Numbers 14

"…don't be afraid of the people of the land. They are only helpless prey to us! They have no protection, but the LORD is with us! Don't be afraid of them!"

NUMBERS 14:9 NLT

When my father went to be with the Lord, I thought that God would send us a senior pastor with a dynamic personality, a booming voice, and several academic degrees. I was looking around, thinking, *Where is he?* The whole time, on the inside I could hear that still small voice saying, "Joel, this is your time. The promise is in you." I said, "God, I don't have the booming voice, the dynamic personality, or the degrees." God said, "Joel, I formed you before the foundation of the world. I put in you everything that you need. I wouldn't ask you to do it if you didn't already have what it takes." I stepped up, and I discovered *I* was the answer to my prayer.

Maybe you're praying for another person to come along and bring your dreams to pass. God is saying, "You're the answer to your prayer. You're equipped and anointed; you can do something great." As with Sarah, just because we don't believe it's going to happen, God doesn't change His mind. Sarah waited a dozen or so years to give birth to Isaac. You are still going to give birth to everything that God has placed in your heart.

This is what Caleb did. He and Joshua were two of the twelve men whom Moses sent in to spy out the Promised Land. They came back and said, "We are well able to take the land; let us go in at once." They knew the promise was in them, but the other ten spies' negative report convinced the entire nation of Israel that they could not defeat their enemies, and they never entered the Promised Land.

Forty years later, when Caleb was eighty-five years old, he knew the promise was still in him. He went back to the place he'd been forty years earlier, and he declared, "Give me this mountain." That mountain had three fierce giants living on it—the giants the other ten spies said made them feel like grasshoppers. It would have been a lot easier to ask for a mountain with less opposition. But at eighty-five years old, he drove out the giants, took the mountain, and saw the dream come to pass.

Today's Prayer
Heavenly Father, thank You that whether Your promise is fulfilled in my life today or ten years from now, You will bring it to pass in Your perfect time, and You will not change Your mind. Thank You that I too can say, "God, give me this mountain." I believe that every giant, those things that are against Your promises, will be conquered. In Jesus' Name. Amen.

Today's Thought
Get your fire back, get your dreams back. Have the same attitude as Caleb: *God, this is what You promised me, and I'm not going to settle for mediocrity when I know You put greatness in me. Yes, it's been a long time. I've gone through disappointments. But God, I still believe the promise is in me.*

DAY 7

Don't Be Surprised
by Opposition

Scripture Reading: 1 Peter 4

*Friends, when life gets really difficult, don't jump
to the conclusion that God isn't on the job. Instead,
be glad that you are in the very thick of what Christ
experienced. This is a spiritual refining process,
with glory just around the corner.*

1 PETER 4:12–13 MSG

My brother, Paul, is a surgeon and spends several months a year in Africa performing operations in small villages. One of the safari guides told him that when a gazelle or a wildebeest is pregnant and about to give birth, a lion will closely stalk that animal. Day after day, the lion will follow the pregnant mother, waiting for her to go into labor. The lion knows that when she goes into labor, she's an easy target, because she can't defend herself. So the lion will actually wait for the mother to go into labor and then not only attack and kill her, but the baby as well.

It's the same principle in life. You will face your greatest attacks when you're about to give birth to the dreams God placed in your heart. The enemy waits until you're close to the promotion, close to the breakthrough. He'll strike when you're just about to step up to a new level. Don't be surprised if you face opposition or you go through a disappointment. Perhaps a friend whom you were counting on is not there. Or it's taking longer than you expected. That simply means you're about to give birth to what God has placed in your heart. The good news is the forces that are for you are greater than the forces that are against you. Your destiny cannot be stopped by a bad break, by disappointments, by opposition, or by other people. God has the final say. He says, "No weapon formed against you will ever prosper."

You may be facing big challenges, things are coming against you. That's a sign you're about to see a dream come to pass. Now is not the time to get discouraged. Now is the time to dig your heels in and declare, "I am in it to win it. I know the promise is in me. I'm not going to let this disappointment, this setback, or this person steal my destiny. I'm going to give birth to everything that God has placed in my heart."

Today's Prayer

Father, thank You that no weapon formed against
me is going to prosper. Thank You that the opposition
I feel is only a sign that I'm about to see the dream come
to pass. I rejoice in what You are doing in my spirit,
that together we are involved in a refining process;
and I believe that glory is just around the corner.
In Jesus' Name. Amen.

Today's Thought

When the going gets tough, you're close to your
breakthrough. You're close to seeing the problem
turn around. You're close to meeting the right person.
God began a good work in you and He
is going to complete it.

God Has a Way

Scripture Reading: Acts 2

*"The promise is for you and your children and
for all who are far off—for all whom the
Lord our God will call."*

Acts 2:39

Troy came from a single-parent home. His family had been through many struggles. His mother became ill and had to have brain surgery. During a huge flood, they lost everything. It was one bad break after another. It didn't look as though Troy would ever get the opportunity to do anything great. The odds were against him. But Troy always had a big dream for his life. When he was in the third grade, he wrote in a school paper that he was going to get a scholarship to go to college. Even as a young boy, he could feel the promise in him to go further, to leave his mark. His dream was to go to Georgetown University, to get a doctorate in international relations, and to become secretary of state of the United States.

For Troy's single-parent mother, that level of education seemed impossible. Troy could have thought, *Too bad for me. I've got a big dream, but I don't have the money. I don't have the connections.* But Troy's attitude was, *The promise is in me. What God has spoken over my life will come to pass.* Those are the better thoughts he needed. He didn't sit back and expect God to do it all for him. He excelled in school. He took college courses in the tenth grade. He graduated number two in his high school class. Troy received not just one scholarship; he was awarded nine scholarships that were worth over one million dollars. His bachelor's degree, his master's, and his doctoral studies are totally paid for at Georgetown University.

What God has promised you, He will bring to pass. You may not see a way, but God has a way. If you'll be the best that you can be, right where you are, God will get you to where He wants you to be.

Today's Prayer
Father in heaven, thank You that when I don't see a way for Your promise to come to pass in my life, You always still have a way. Thank You that Your promise is for me and in me. I believe that what You have spoken over my life will come to pass. In Jesus' Name. Amen.

Today's Thought
There is a force in you that is more powerful than any opposition. Greater is He that is in you than anything that comes against you. When you press past what's coming against you, on the other side of that difficulty is a new level of your destiny.

A Fire Shut Up in Your Bones

Scripture Reading: Jeremiah 20

[God, Your] word is in my heart like a fire,
a fire shut up in my bones. I am weary of holding
it in; indeed, I cannot.

JEREMIAH 20:9

In the Scripture, God put a promise in Jeremiah that he would be a prophet and speak to the nations. Jeremiah was young, afraid, and he didn't think he could do it (see Jer. 1). People and obstacles came against him. He got so discouraged that he was about to give up. Eventually, Jeremiah began to tell God how bad it was. He listed one complaint after another. "God, these people are mocking me. When I speak, they make fun of me. I'm being ridiculed. I'm tired. I'm lonely. I'm intimidated." Jeremiah had a long list.

But just when you thought Jeremiah was going to quit, he said, "God, I feel like giving up, but Your word in my heart is like a fire shut up in my bones." He was saying, "God, I don't see how it can happen. All the odds are against me. But this promise You put in me will not go away. It's like fire. It's like a burning. I can't get away from it." When Jeremiah began to think better and let the fire burn, his life passion was restored.

You may be at a place where you can easily be discouraged and give up on what God has placed in your heart. But the good news is, as was true for Jeremiah, there is a fire shut up in your bones. There is a promise that God has spoken over you that will not die. You can try to ignore it. Your mind or others will try to convince you it's never going to happen. But deep down, you'll feel a burning, a restlessness, a fire. That's the promise God put in you. God loves you too much to let you remain average. He's going to push you into greatness. You're going to accomplish more than you thought possible. You're going to go further than you dreamed. You're going to see the exceeding greatness of God's power. What He's spoken over your life will come to pass.

You don't need anyone else to give birth to what God has placed in your heart. Quit looking for the other person. You are the right person. You have what it takes. Now stir up what's on the inside. It's time for you to do something great!

Today's Prayer

Father, thank You for the fire of the promise that is burning deep inside my life. Help me to stir up the fire of faith in Your promises and let the passion become a flame. I believe that I am going to see the exceeding greatness of Your power helping me accomplish more than I thought possible. In Jesus' Name. Amen.

Today's Thought

You have to stir up your faith. There is a flame that is alive on the inside of you. You are equipped. You are anointed. It's time for you to be celebrated. It's time for you to rise to a new level.

Ask Big

A God of Abundance

Scripture Reading: Matthew 14

You anoint my head with oil; my cup overflows.

PSALM 23:5

When God laid out the plan for your life, He didn't just put into it what you need to get by to survive, to endure until the end. He put more than enough in it. He's a God of abundance. We see this all through the Scripture. After Jesus multiplied the little boy's lunch of five loaves of bread and two fish, thousands of people ate, and yet there were twelve basketfuls of leftovers. It is interesting that they had counted the people beforehand, so Jesus knew how many people were in the crowd that day. If He had wanted to be exact, He could have made just enough so there would be no leftovers. On purpose, He made more than enough. That's the God we serve.

David said, "My cup overflows." He had an abundance, more than he needed. Yes, we should thank God that our needs are supplied. We should be grateful that we have enough, but don't settle there. That's not your destiny. He is a more-than-enough God. He wants you to have an abundance, so that you can be a blessing to those around you.

This is where the Israelites missed it. They had been in slavery for so many years that they became conditioned to not having enough, to barely getting by. When Pharaoh got upset with Moses, he told his foremen to have the Israelites make the same amount of bricks without the hay and straw being provided for them. I'm sure the Israelites prayed, "God, please, help us to make our quotas. God, please, help us to find the supplies that we need." They prayed from a slave mentality, from a limited mind-set. Instead of asking to be freed from their oppressors, they were asking to become better slaves. Instead of praying for what God promised them, the land flowing with milk and honey, they prayed that God would help them function better in their dysfunction.

Are you asking today to become a better slave or are you asking for the abundant, overflowing, more-than-enough life that God has for you? God says you are to reign in life, that you are blessed and you cannot be cursed, that whatever you touch will prosper and succeed. Don't pray to just get by, to endure. Dare to ask big. Ask for what God has promised you.

Today's Prayer
Heavenly Father, thank You that You are El Shaddai, the God of More Than Enough, not the God of Barely Enough. You are the God of Overflow and Abundance. I ask You for the overflowing, more-than-enough life that You have for me. In Jesus' Name. Amen.

Today's Thought
Take the limits off God and ask big, not from a slave mentality, not from a limited mind-set. Don't ask God to help you function better in your dysfunction. Ask God to help you think bigger and better so you can live better. Ask Him for your dream.

More Than Enough

Scripture Reading: Psalm 35

Let them say continually, "Let the LORD be magnified,
who has pleasure in the prosperity of His servant."

PSALM 35:27 NKJV

A lady whom I know has four small grandchildren whom she ended up having to raise. She wasn't planning on it, but something happened with her daughter. At first, she was a little discouraged, not knowing how it was going to work out. Three of the children were in an expensive private school, and the grandmother didn't have the funds to keep paying their tuition. She could've prayed from a slave mentality: "God, this isn't fair. Please just help us to survive." Instead, she had the boldness to ask big: "God, I don't have the required funds, but You own it all. You're a God of abundance. And, God, I'm asking You to make a way, even though I don't see how it can ever happen."

At the end of the children's first school year, she owed a small amount on tuition, so she went to the school to pay. The secretary called up her records on the computer and said, "No, you don't owe anything. Everything's paid up."

"That can't be," the grandmother responded. "I have the notice right here. This says that I owe this amount."

The secretary said, "No, ma'am. It says right here that all three of the children's tuitions have been paid, not only for the rest of this year, but all the way through the eighth grade." An anonymous donor had prepaid it for years to come!

God can make things happen that you could never make happen. He's already placed abundance in your future. He's already lined up the right people, the breaks you need, doors to open that you could never open. My question is, "Are you asking big?" Or are you letting your circumstances—how you were raised, what somebody said—talk you out of it? If you go through life praying only "barely getting by" prayers, you'll miss the fullness of your destiny.

When you get this in your spirit, that the God who breathed life into you, the God who called you, set you apart, and crowned you with favor, is a more-than-enough God, an abundant God, an overflowing God, you'll have a boldness to ask for big things.

Today's Prayer

Father, thank You that You take pleasure in providing for my prosperity and health and well-being. Thank You for challenging me to believe that You are my more-than-enough God and to ask for big things. I believe that You have already placed abundance in my future and crowned me with favor. In Jesus' Name. Amen.

Today's Thought

Don't ask to just manage the addiction; ask to be free from the addiction. Don't ask to just pay your bills; ask to be totally out of debt, so you can be a blessing to others. Don't ask to just see your child get back on the right course; ask that God will use him to make his mark on this generation.

What Is It That You Want?

Scripture Reading: Matthew 20

*The crowd rebuked [the blind men] and told
them to be quiet, but they shouted all the louder,
"Lord, Son of David, have mercy on us!" Jesus
stopped and called them. "What do you want
me to do for you?" he asked.*

MATTHEW 20:31–32

Matthew 20 records the story of Jesus walking through a town where there were two blind men by the side of the road. When they heard all the commotion and that Jesus was passing by, they started shouting, "Jesus, have mercy on us!" Jesus walked over to them and said, "What do you want me to do for you?" It seemed like a strange question. It's obvious what they needed. They were blind. Why did Jesus ask them? Because He wanted to see what they were believing. They could've said, "Jesus, we just need some help out here. We're blind. We just need a little better place to live or some cash for some food." If they had asked from a limited mentality, it would have kept them in defeat. Instead, they asked big. They said, "Lord, we want to see. We want our eyes to be opened." They were saying, "We know You can do the impossible." When Jesus heard their request, He touched their eyes, and instantly they could see.

God is asking us the same thing He asked those two blind men: "What is it that you want Me to do for you?" Now, how You answer is going to have a great impact on what God does. Don't say, "God, I just want to make it through this year. Have You seen what apartments are renting for these days?" "God, my family's so dysfunctional, just help us to survive." "God, I don't like my job. Just help me to endure it." That is going to limit your destiny.

Do what those blind men did. Dare to ask big. "God, I want to be free from this addiction." "God, I want to meet the right person." "God, I want to see my whole family serve You." "God, I want to start my own business." Ask for your dreams. Ask even for things that seem impossible.

Today's Prayer
Father in heaven, thank You that just as You restored the sight of the blind men, You can do the impossible in my life. Thank You that Your blessings are chasing me down. I believe that You are bringing the desires of my heart to me. In Jesus' Name. Amen.

Today's Thought
Your dream may look impossible. Turn it around with some better thoughts: *God, You said Your blessings would chase me down, that I'm surrounded by favor, that goodness and mercy are following me, and that You would give me the desires of my heart.*

Take the Limits Off

Scripture Reading: James 4

*You do not have because you do not ask. You
ask and do not receive, because you ask amiss,
that you may spend it on your pleasures.*

JAMES 4:2–3 NKJV

The Scripture says, "You ask and do not receive, because you
ask amiss." That word *amiss* in the original language means
"sick, weak, miserable." When we ask to become better slaves,
that's a sick prayer. When we ask to get by, to endure, to barely
make it, that's a weak prayer. That's asking amiss. God is saying,
"I created the whole universe. I own it all. Don't come to Me
with a sick prayer, a weak prayer, asking Me to help you live
in mediocrity, endure the trouble, and survive another month.
When you come to Me, ask big, knowing that I'm a God of
more than enough." He's saying, "Ask Me to show out in your
life. Ask Me to heal you from that disease. Ask Me to accelerate
your goals."

When you ask big, God calls that a healthy prayer. That's
when He says to the angels, "Go to work. Release My favor.
Loose those chains. Open up new doors." "Well, Joel, I'm just
praying that I'll make it through these tough times. Business
is really slow." May I say this respectfully? That's a sick prayer.
That prayer has the flu! "I'm just praying that I'll learn how
to manage this addiction. Grandmother had it. Mother had it.
Now I do, too." That's a weak prayer. Your attitude should be,
*God, this addiction keeps getting passed down through my family
line, but I believe this is a new day and that You've raised me up*

to put a stop to it—that I will be the one to break the generational curse and start the generational blessing.

Don't ask to become a better slave. Ask to be the difference maker. Ask to set a new standard. When you say, "God, help me to get that scholarship so I can go to college," that's not just being hopeful, just being positive. That's your faith being released. That's what allows God to do great things. Or, "God, I don't have the funds for the building project just yet, but, Lord, I want to thank You that opportunity is headed my way, that blessings are chasing me down." No more sick prayers. Take the limits off God. Ask big.

Today's Prayer

Father, thank You that You want to do great things in
my life so that You will be glorified in how I spend all
that You provide, in fulfilling my life purpose, in blessing
others through me as You have blessed me. Thank You
that as I pray in faith for Your best, You are propelling me
into my destiny. I believe that You will do great
things. In Jesus' Name. Amen.

Today's Thought

This is the year for God to show out in your life, to
accelerate His goodness, to propel you into your destiny.
Ask Him for new levels. Ask Him for explosive blessings.
Ask Him to propel you into your purpose.

DAY 5

No More Weak, Sick Prayers

Scripture Reading: Acts 4

Jabez cried out to the God of Israel, "Oh, that you would bless me and enlarge my territory! Let your hand be with me, and keep me from harm so that I will be free from pain." And God granted his request.

1 CHRONICLES 4:10

This is what a man by the name of Jabez did in the Scripture. His name literally means "pain, sorrow, suffering." Every time someone said, "Hello, Jabez," they were saying "Hello, trouble." "Hello, sorrow." "Hello, pain." They were prophesying defeat and failure. You can imagine how he could have let that keep him in mediocrity, make him feel inferior and insecure. There was something different about Jabez, though. Despite what people labeled him, he looked up to the heavens and said, "God, I'm asking You to bless me indeed." He could have just said, "God, bless me." That would've been okay. But he had the boldness to ask big.

Jabez was a man who was supposed to have trouble and heartache, to live depressed and defeated, but he shook off the slave mentality. His attitude was, *It doesn't matter what people say about me. It doesn't matter what my circumstances look like. I know who I am—a child of the Most High God.* He went on to say, "God, enlarge my territories." He was saying, "God, help me to go beyond the norm. Let me see abundance. Let me see more of Your favor." I'm sure thoughts told him, "Jabez, God's not going to bless you. You come from the wrong family. Your own parents labeled you 'sorrow, pain, trouble.'" But people don't determine your destiny; God does. The Scripture says that God granted Jabez his request. God blessed him indeed.

Like Jabez, you may have plenty of reasons to settle where you are—what you didn't get, what people said, how impossible it looks. The odds may be against you, but the good news is that God is for you. He is more powerful than any force that's trying to stop you. He knows how to make up for what you didn't get. He can thrust you further than you ever imagined, but you have to do as Jabez did and pray bold prayers. Ask in spite of what the circumstances look like. Ask in spite of what people are telling you. Ask in spite of what the enemy keeps whispering in your ear.

Today's Prayer

Heavenly Father, thank You that when the odds are all against me, You are for me. Thank You that nothing and no one is more powerful than You and that I can dare to pray bold prayers. I believe that You are blessing me as You did Jabez and enlarging my territory.
In Jesus' Name. Amen.

Today's Thought

Jabez could have prayed a weak, sick prayer and thought, *God, I've had a rough upbringing. I'm just asking You to help me survive.* If he had done that, we wouldn't be talking about him today. If you're going to beat the odds, stand out in the crowd, and reach your highest potential, you have to learn this principle of asking big.

DAY 6

Today Is Your Birthday

Scripture Reading: Psalm 2

*"You're my son, and today is your birthday.
What do you want? Name it: Nations as a present?
Continents as a prize? You can command
them all to dance for you..."*

PSALM 2:7–9 MSG

Did you notice how big God thinks? Sometimes we're praying for a three dollar-an-hour raise; God's talking about giving you nations. We're praying for a promotion; God's got a business for you to own. We're praying to pay our bills; God's planning on blessing you so you can pay other people's bills. We're looking at the five loaves and two fish; God's thinking about the twelve basketfuls of leftovers.

What does that mean, "Today is your birthday"? On your birthday, more than at any other time, you feel entitled to ask for something out of the ordinary. Normally, you don't want anybody to go out of the way for you, but on your birthday, you think, *Okay, I'm going to ask for a new outfit or for a set of golf clubs.* Over time, as we get older, our enthusiasm may go down a little, but think back to when you were a child. You knew that was your special day. You had the boldness to ask for what you really wanted.

A while ago, a little boy came up to me out in the hallway. He's five years old, and I see him at the church all the time. He came running up, so excited, and exclaimed, "It's my birthday today!" I gave him a big hug and told him, "Happy birthday!" I walked about five steps away, and he came back and grabbed my leg and said it again: "It's my birthday!" I thought, *I know, you just told me.* We hugged and did it all again as though it was the first time. This happened again and again. About the seventh time, instead of telling me it was his birthday, he looked up and said, "What are you going to get me for my birthday?" The reason he kept coming back is because he felt entitled to a present. He knew it was his special day.

God is saying, "When you pray, act as though it's your birthday. Come to Me with a boldness. Ask Me for what you really want. Don't hold back. Tell Me your dreams. Tell Me what you're believing for. Ask for the secret things I placed in your heart."

Today's Prayer
Father, thank You for declaring that this day and every day is my birthday and for inviting me to come to You with boldness and to ask for what I want. Help me to think big. I open my heart and believe You will move heaven and earth to bring about Your destiny for me. In Jesus' Name. Amen.

Today's Thought
You are God's biggest deal. You're the apple of His eye. You're His most prized possession. Ask Him for your dreams. You're not inconveniencing God. God will move heaven and earth to bring about His destiny in your life. Dare to ask big.

DAY 7

It Is Your Father's
Good Pleasure

Scripture Reading: Luke 12

*"Do not fear, little flock, for it is your Father's
good pleasure to give you the kingdom."*

LUKE 12:32 NKJV

In yesterday's Scripture verse, God says, "Today is your birthday. What do you want?" Too often, instead of approaching God as though it's our birthday, believing that He'll do something special, we do just the opposite. "Joel, I can't ask for what I really want. That wouldn't be right. That would be selfish." The Scripture says it is the Father's good pleasure to give you the kingdom. Nothing makes God happier than for Him to see you step up to who you were created to be. Notice, today is always in the present. When you get up tomorrow morning, God is saying, "Today is your birthday." Two weeks from now, "Today is your birthday." Seven years from now, "Today is your birthday."

When I received word that the Compaq Center was coming available, something ignited on the inside of me. I knew it was supposed to be ours, but every voice said, "It's never going to happen. It's too big, Joel. You don't deserve it. Who do you think you are to even ask for it?" Instead of believing those lies, I did what I'm asking you to do. I went to God as though it was my birthday, and I said, "God, I know this is far out. Normally, I'd never ask for it, but, God, I believe You put this in our path. This is part of my destiny. So, God, I'm asking You to make a way, even though I don't see a way."

What is interesting is that in all the big things I've ever asked God for, I've never once felt as though He said, "Joel, you've got a lot of nerve. What are you doing, asking for that?" Just the opposite. In my heart, I can feel God whispering, "Joel, I love the fact that you dare to ask big. I love the fact that you believe I can do the impossible." Of course, everything I've asked for hasn't come to pass, but the point is, if you go to God with childlike faith, believing that it's your birthday, asking for things that you wouldn't normally ask for, there will be times when you see God show out in your life in ways greater than you ever imagined.

Today's Prayer

Father in heaven, thank You for the beautiful promise
that it is Your good pleasure to give me the kingdom.
Thank You for encouraging me to dare to ask big.
I believe and declare that this is my birthday and I am
asking You to show out through my life in ways
I never imagined. In Jesus' Name. Amen.

Today's Thought

Every morning when you get up, just imagine God
saying, "Happy birthday, Son." "Happy birthday,
Daughter." Why does He do this? So you'll have the
boldness to ask your heavenly Father for things
that you wouldn't normally ask for.

DAY 8

Stand Out and Make a Difference

Scripture Reading: Psalm 72

*May all kings bow down to him and all nations
serve him. For he will deliver the needy who cry out,
the afflicted who have no one to help.*

PSALM 72:11–12

In Psalm 72, King Solomon prayed what seemed to be a very
self-centered prayer. He asked God to make him well-known,
that his fame would spread throughout the land, that the wealth
and honor of other nations would be brought to him, and that
kings and queens would bow down before him. You would
think God would say, "Solomon, I'm not going to make you
famous. I'm not going to give you honor, wealth, and influence.
You need to learn some humility." But God didn't rebuke him
or tell him he was selfish and greedy. God did exactly what he
asked for. Solomon became one of the most famous people of
his day. The queen of Sheba came, bowed down before him,
and brought him gold and silver.

Here's the key: The reason God answered that bold prayer
is because Solomon went on to pray, "God, if You'll make my
name famous, if You'll give me influence and wealth, I will use
it to help the widows, to take care of the orphans, to bring
justice to the oppressed, to give a voice to those who don't have
any voice." He asked big, not just so he would look impressive
and live in the biggest palace. It was so he could lift the fallen,
restore the broken, and help the hurting to advance God's kingdom. God has no problem giving you influence, honor, wealth,

and even fame, as long as your dream, in some way, is connected to helping others, to making this world a better place. When your thoughts align with God's thoughts for others, He will help make your life better.

God is raising up a new generation of Solomons, people who have the boldness to say, "God, make me famous in my field. Let my gifts and talents stand out. Let my work be so excellent, so inspiring, that people all around me know who I am, not for my glory, but so I can use my influence to advance Your kingdom." Whatever field you're in—medicine, sales, construction, accounting, teaching—I dare you to pray, "God, make me famous in my field. Let me shine. Give me influence."

Today's Prayer
Father, thank You that You want my life to lift the fallen, to restore the broken, and to help the hurting. I want in every way possible to advance Your kingdom and bring glory to Your name. I ask You to give me influence and make me famous in my field. In Jesus' Name. Amen.

——————————

Today's Thought
You are not limited by who you know, by how influential you are, or by how much income you have. There's no limit to what God will do for you if you'll use what He's given you to help others.

DAY 9

Help Others along the Way

Scripture Reading: 1 Kings 10

*"I will open the windows of heaven for you. I will
pour out a blessing so great you won't have enough
room to take it in! Try it! Put me to the test!"*

<small>MALACHI 3:10 NLT</small>

One time, I was playing basketball with some friends, and I had to leave early to go to a doctor's appointment. A teammate of mine works in the medical field, and he asked me who I was going to see. I said, "Dr. Price, a friend of mine."

He looked up and said, "*The* Dr. Price?"

"No, *just* Dr. Price," I replied. "I've known him for thirty years."

"Is he *the* Dr. Price who's in infectious medicine?"

"Yes, that's him," I said.

"Oh, man," he exclaimed, "he's the best! He's famous. People come to see him from all over."

I mentioned earlier what Dr. Price does with his "fame," his wealth, and his influence—he uses it to help needy people in third-world countries. Dr. Price never dreamed he would be where he is today. God made him famous in his field.

I wonder what would happen if you would dare to pray, "God, make me famous. God, cause me to stand out so I can make a big difference in this world." If you're an architect, dare to pray, "God, give me ideas, creativity, and designs that stand out." Then use your influence to design a boys' home or an orphanage. If you're a mechanic, dare to pray, "God, make me famous. Let me be so skilled and have so much expertise that people come to me to see how it's done." Then use your influence to fix the cars of single moms, to mentor young men and teach them how to do it.

If you'll do this, I believe and declare, as He did for Solomon, God is going to give you more influence, more resources, and more notoriety. Now, do your part. No more sick prayers. No more weak prayers. Get rid of that slave mentality. Go to God as though it's your birthday. Ask Him for your dreams. As Jabez did, dare to say, "God, bless me indeed." You're going to accomplish your dreams, rise higher than you ever thought possible, and become everything God created you to be.

Today's Prayer

Heavenly Father, thank You that You are making things happen around me that I could never make happen on my own, without Your equipping power. Thank You that You have the power to make me stand out so I can make a difference in the world. I believe that You will use and increase my influence to help others.
In Jesus' Name. Amen.

Today's Thought

God can make things happen that you could never make happen. He'll cause you to stand out so you can use your influence, not only to reach your goals, but so you can help others along the way.

You Have What You Need

DAY 1

You Are Lacking Nothing

Scripture Reading: Psalm 34

Those who trust in the LORD will lack no good thing.

PSALM 34:10 NLT

So often we think, *If I had more money, I could accomplish my dreams. If I had a bigger house, I'd be happy. If I had more talent, a better personality, and if I knew the right people, I could do something great.* But as long as you feel as though you're lacking, you don't have enough, and you were shortchanged, you'll make excuses to be less than your best.

You have to get a new perspective. God has given you exactly what you need for the season you're in. You have the talent, the friends, the connections, the resources, and the experience you need for right now. It doesn't mean that's all you're ever going to have. You may need more next month or next year. When that time comes, God will make sure that you have more then.

Scripture says, "Those who trust in the Lord will never lack any good thing." Because your trust is in the Lord, you don't have to worry. Whatever you need, God will make sure you have it when you need it. You won't lack any good thing. This means that if you don't have it right now, don't be discouraged. You don't need it right now. Our attitude should be, *I'm equipped, empowered, and anointed for this moment. I am not lacking, shortchanged, inadequate, missing out, or less than. I have what I need for today.*

This approach is so much better than thinking, *If I just had the finances…If the loan would have gone through…If she would have been my friend…If I had a better personality…* If you needed a better personality, God would have given you a better personality. God wasn't having a bad day when He created you. If you needed more talent, God would have given you more talent. If you needed more friends, you would have more friends. Take what you have and make the most of it. It's what you need for right now.

This is an empowering way to live. You're not making excuses. You're not feeling shortchanged. You're thinking better, so you'll live better.

Today's Prayer
Father, thank You for the assurance that You have provided me with exactly what I need for the season I am in. Thank You that You have equipped and empowered me with every good thing right now. I believe You will keep providing for me as I need it. In Jesus' Name. Amen.

Today's Thought
The truth is, God has already lined up the right people, the right opportunities, the finances, the wisdom, the good breaks, and the protection you need. It's in your present, it's in your future. As long as you keep honoring God, He will give you what you need when you need it.

Will You Trust Him?

Scripture Reading: Isaiah 45

*"I will give you hidden treasures, riches stored in secret places, so that you may know that I am the L*ORD*, the God of Israel, who summons you by name."*

ISAIAH 45:3

Years ago I used to think, *If we had a bigger building…If we had more members…If I could minister better…If I had more experience…* There was always something I didn't have or I couldn't do, always some reason I couldn't feel good about myself. If I hadn't changed those thoughts, they would have put limits on how I lived.

One day I realized what I'm telling you: I have what I need for the season I'm in right now. I have the strength that I need for today. It may not be enough strength for tomorrow, but that's okay. When tomorrow comes, God will give me strength for that day. I have the talent, the qualifications, and the experience I need for right now. It may not be as much as somebody else has, but that's okay. I'm not competing with them. I'm competing with myself to become the best me that I can possibly be.

Several years ago, someone published an article that talked about how I haven't been to seminary and how I wasn't qualified to lead a large ministry. At first that bothered me. Then I read Galatians 1, where the apostle Paul, who wrote about half the books of the New Testament, said, "I was not appointed by any group or by human authority…my call came from God who raised Jesus from the dead."

People may not approve you. Don't worry about it. God

approves you. People didn't call you. People don't determine your destiny. People can't stop God's plan for your life. God called you. God equipped you. God anointed you. When you come to the end of your life, you don't have to answer to people. You'll answer to Almighty God. Don't let what some person says or does make you feel less than or unqualified. You've been handpicked by the Creator of the universe. You are lacking nothing for the season that you're in right now. Now quit thinking about all the things that you don't have and all the things that you wish were different.

Today's Prayer

Father in heaven, thank You that You know me by name
and that Your call upon my life is not subject to other
people's approval. Thank You that You have freed me
to live for You and to become the best me that I can
possibly be. I trust in You with my whole heart.
In Jesus' Name. Amen.

Today's Thought

My question is, "Will you trust Him?" Will you keep
a good attitude and be your best, even though it's
taking longer than you expected, even though the problem
hasn't turned around, and even though a dream hasn't
come to pass? If you will be faithful where you are now,
knowing that you have exactly what you need
for the season that you're in, God will get you
to where you're supposed to be.

DAY 3

Much, Much More

Scripture Reading: 2 Samuel 12

"[David,] if that had not been enough, I would have given you much, much more."

2 Samuel 12:8 NLT

In the book of 2 Samuel is the story of how King David got off course with his life. The prophet Nathan was correcting him. In doing so, he reminded David of what God had brought him through. David had experienced God's goodness, favor, protection, provision, and healing down through the years. God made an interesting statement through Nathan: "David, if it had not been enough, I would have given you much, much more." In other words, "David, looking back over your life, if you were ever lacking, if you ever needed more wisdom, more favor, more protection, or more finance, God would have given it to you."

That tells me that what I have right now is what I need to fulfill my destiny. The moment it becomes insufficient is the moment God will give me more. The moment something starts to keep you from your destiny, the moment it begins to stop God's plan for your life, is the moment God will show up, the moment He will intervene. So if it hasn't happened yet, don't be discouraged, thinking that it's never going to work out. If it hasn't happened, you haven't needed it. When you need it, it won't be one second late.

"But, Joel, all I have is this old car. I'm depressed." Have a new attitude and say, "This old car is all I need right now. God is on the throne directing my steps. When I need more, He will give me more."

"All I have is this one friend." Turn it around. "This one friend is all I need for this season. When I need more friends, God will give me more friends."

"If I just had more money…" If you needed more money to fulfill your destiny right now and God withheld it, He wouldn't be a just God.

"All I have is this low-level job." Tell yourself, "That's all I need right now. When it's my time to be promoted, nothing can stand against my God. I will be promoted. But in the meantime, I'm going to keep being my best right where I am."

Today's Prayer

Father, thank You for the amazing "much, much more" promise that You made to David and to me as well. Thank You that I have everything I need right now to fulfill my destiny, to live a life that brings pleasure to You. I believe that You are on the throne and nothing I need will be a minute late. In Jesus' Name. Amen.

Today's Thought

The moment you need a new friend, the moment you need a good break, the moment you need an idea, it will show up. God is closely watching your life. You are His most prized possession. He is saying to you what He said to David: "If it's ever not enough, you can count on Me. I will always be there to give you more."

DAY 4

Not One Second Late

Scripture Reading: Isaiah 35

"See, I have engraved you on the palms of my hands..."

Isaiah 49:16

In 1959, my father was the pastor of a large denominational church. They had nearly a thousand members and had just built a beautiful new sanctuary. Back then, that was a big deal. My father's future looked very bright. But through a series of events, the day came when he knew he was supposed to leave that church and start Lakewood. It didn't make sense from a practical standpoint. He didn't have a building or any organization backing him up. Most of his friends didn't support him. He could have made a list of all the things he didn't have. If he had stayed focused on that, he would never have moved off dead center.

But my father took a step of faith and started Lakewood with ninety people in an old, run-down feed store. Instead of thinking, *All I have are these ninety people,* his attitude was, *These ninety people are all I need.* Instead of thinking, *All I have is this old feed store,* his better thought was, *This old feed store is all I need.* When you realize the Creator of the universe is directing your steps, giving you what you need, and that the moment it becomes inadequate, He promises to show up and give you more, you won't go around discouraged, thinking, *This is not fair. Why don't I get any good breaks? When is this ever going to change?* You'll just keep being your best, honoring God.

That's what my father did and today, over fifty-seven years later, Lakewood is still going strong. Maybe you're discouraged because of what has not happened in your life. You're wondering when the situation is going to turn around, when you're going to get that good break. Quit being stressed over it. God has you in the palm of His hands. He has written every day of your life in His book. God knows what you need and when you need it, and He knows how to get it to you. If you don't have something right now, you didn't miss it. You didn't get shortchanged. God didn't forget about you. As long as you're honoring Him, at the right time, when you need something or someone, the right thing or person will show up.

Today's Prayer

Heavenly Father, thank You that I have been engraved on the palms of Your hands. Thank You that You know what I need and when I need it as well as how to get it to me. I choose to stop stressing out over what I don't have, knowing it will be here when I really need it. In Jesus' Name. Amen.

Today's Thought

When you need it, the finances will come. When you need it, the healing, the restoration, and the vindication will find you. If it hasn't happened yet, don't sit around being sour. Have the attitude, *I don't need it. When I need it, God promises it won't be one second late.*

You and God Are a Majority

Scripture Reading: John 4

Jesus answered her, "If you knew the gift of God and who it is that asks you for a drink, you would have asked him and he would have given you living water."

JOHN 4:10

The Scripture tells the story of how Jesus met a Samaritan woman at a well and asked her for something to drink. She was surprised because in those days the Jews didn't have anything to do with the Samaritans, let alone a Jewish man speaking with a Samaritan woman. She said, "How can You ask me for something to drink?"

Jesus said, "If you knew who I am, you would ask of Me and I would give you living water."

She immediately began to view the circumstances from a human perspective. She said, "But, sir, You don't have anything to draw water with. You don't have a bucket or a pail. How can You give me living water?"

I wonder how many times we do the same thing. God tells us He is going to do something great in our lives. Down deep, He puts a dream on the inside that we're going to rise higher. We're going to see our marriage restored. We're going to get healthy again. We feel it strongly, but as the Samaritan woman did, we start looking at what we don't have, the way we were raised, the obstacles in our path. Before long, we talk ourselves out of it. "I can't do anything great. I don't have the talent. My marriage is too far gone. The medical report is too bad." You're just looking with a limited natural perspective, but we serve a supernatural God. He can take something that is ordinary, breathe on it, and turn it into something that's extraordinary. You may have average talent, but when God breathes on your life, you will go further than people who have great talent. Don't talk yourself out of it.

Don't underestimate what you have. It may look small and insignificant. Compared to what you're facing, perhaps it seems utterly useless. All the odds are against you. But you and God are a majority. God can open doors that should have never opened in the natural. God can take you beyond where your talent and your education say you should be. God can make a way even when you don't see a way.

Today's Prayer
Father, You are the only One who can give me the
living water that so satisfies me that I never thirst again.
Thank You that You are breathing into my life and
changing me into someone extraordinary to do
the extraordinary. I believe that You and I are
a majority. In Jesus' Name. Amen.

Today's Thought
The Creator of the universe is breathing on your life. He
is breathing on your health, breathing on your finances,
breathing on your marriage. If you will be confident in
what God has given you, He can take what looks
like little and turn it into much.

Use What You've Been Given

Scripture Reading: John 6

*Andrew, Simon Peter's brother, spoke up,
"Here is a boy with five small barley loaves
and two small fish, but how far will
they go among so many?"*

JOHN 6:8–9

On one occasion, Jesus had been teaching thousands of people. It was getting late in the day and everyone was hungry. Jesus turned to His disciples and said, "I want you to feed all these people." They didn't have any food out there in the wilderness. There were no grocery stores. On the surface, it seemed as though what Jesus asked was impossible. But here's the key: God will never ask you to do something and then not give you the ability to do it. "I can't raise this child, he's too difficult." God wouldn't have given you this child if you weren't able to raise him. "The people at work are driving me crazy." When God gave you that job, He gave you the ability to be there with a good attitude. "I can't accomplish my dreams. I don't know the right people." The moment God put the dream in your heart, He lined up everything you need to bring it to pass.

The disciples said to Jesus, "We can't feed all these people. It's impossible. We don't have any food. Send them away so they can go to the villages and buy food for themselves."

Jesus listened to all their excuses, and finally He said to them, "You've told Me all about what you don't have. All I want to know is what you do have."

They said, "We just have five loaves of bread and two small

fish. But what is this among so many?" They had considered it and dismissed it. It was not enough.

"Joel, I believe I could do something great if I had more going for me, if I had more talent, more friends, and more money." Get rid of the "I don't have enough" mentality. God controls the whole universe. That's the better thought you need.

Jesus took the five loaves and the two fish, prayed over them, and they supernaturally multiplied. That small meal ended up feeding probably fifteen thousand people, plus there were basketfuls of leftovers to take home. That's what happens when you give God what you have. He will multiply it. Are you talking yourself out of something God has put in your heart?

Today's Prayer
Father in heaven, thank You that You take the loaves and the fishes in my life and multiply them whenever I put them into Your hands. Thank You that I can give You my dreams and goals and You will do something great with them. I gladly surrender my life to You today. In Jesus' Name. Amen.

Today's Thought
God is saying to you today what Jesus said to the disciples: "Give Me what you have. Don't make excuses. Don't sit on the sidelines of life feeling intimidated and shortchanged. Put your life, your goals, and your dreams into My hands."

More Than You Can Ask or Think

Scripture Reading: Zechariah 4

"Do not despise these small beginnings, for the
LORD rejoices to see the work begin…"

ZECHARIAH 4:10 NLT

Mary Bethune was born in South Carolina in 1875, the fifteenth of seventeen children. Her parents were former slaves. Despite the odds being against her, she was able to get a good education and even went to college. From the time she was a little girl, her dream was always to teach young people. She was a straight-A student. You couldn't meet a finer young woman. She graduated from college and turned her application in to become a missionary in Africa. Several months later, she got a notification that she had been turned down. For some reason, she wasn't accepted. But instead of sitting around thinking about how badly life was treating her, she had the attitude, *I didn't get that position. I must not have needed it. If it was going to keep me from my destiny, God would have never allowed it.*

Eventually Mary Bethune decided to start her own school. She didn't have any money, or a building, or any supplies or equipment. She found some old cardboard boxes and used them for desks. She would take red berries each day and drain the juice out of them, so her students could use that for ink in their pens. A few years later, a local college noticed what was happening and asked her to join forces with them in what became known as the Bethune-Cookman College. In 1936, President Franklin Roosevelt appointed her as the director of the Division of Negro

Affairs and an advisor to his cabinet on black employment, education, and civil rights issues, making her the first African-American woman ever to become a presidential advisor.

What am I saying? Don't despise the day of small beginnings. Remember, all David had was a slingshot and five smooth stones. It looked insignificant, ordinary, certainly nothing special. But God breathed on him, and he defeated Goliath and became the king of Israel. All Moses had was an ordinary stick, something he found on the ground, yet when he picked up that rod and held it in the air, the Red Sea supernaturally parted.

If you'll use what God has given you, He will multiply it. He will not only bring your dreams to pass, but He will do more than you can ask or think.

Today's Prayer

Father, thank You for Your word to never despise the day of small beginnings, for You rejoice to see me use what You have given me and You will bring the increase as I trust in You. Thank You that a slingshot and five stones are enough to bring down a giant. I believe that nothing can keep me from my destiny. In Jesus' Name. Amen.

Today's Thought

Samson was surrounded by a huge army. Everywhere he looked there were horses, chariots, and weapons. All he had was the jawbone of a donkey. No weapon. No armor. Nobody was backing him up. But he picked up that jawbone, God breathed on him, and he defeated a thousand men. What's in your hand? Whatever it is, it's enough!

DAY 8

The Sound of Footsteps

Scripture Reading: 2 Kings 7

When [the four men with leprosy] reached the edge of the camp, no one was there, for the Lord had caused the Arameans to hear the sound of chariots and horses and a great army...

2 KINGS 7:5–6

The Scripture tells of four lepers who were so desperate for food, they were marching toward the enemy's camp. These four men had nothing: no supplies, no food, no protection, not even their health. In the natural, they didn't have a chance of surviving. They could have been sitting around depressed, focused on what they didn't have. Instead they were using what they did have. As they were marching toward the enemy's camp, God multiplied the sound of their footsteps. It sounded like a huge army was attacking. Their enemies took off running for their lives and left all their supplies behind, saving not only the lepers' lives but the people of Samaria as well.

"Well, Joel, I don't have a lot of talent." Maybe not. But do you have any footsteps? Mary Bethune did not have money, but she had red berries. My father did not have a church building, but he had an old, run-down feed store. If you'll use what God has given you, He will multiply it. He will multiply your talent, multiply your resources, and multiply your influence. God is not into addition. He is into multiplication. What you have today may seem small, but if you'll keep honoring God, it's not going to stay small. You're going to come into supernatural increase, good breaks, divine connections, and opportunities that you've never seen before. You have exactly what you need to fulfill your destiny. Now here's the key: You may not have as much as another family member, a coworker, or a friend. But that's okay. You're not running their race. You're running your race. If God gave you what they have, it wouldn't help you. It would hinder you. You're not anointed to be them. You're anointed to be you.

Don't dismiss what God has given you. It may not seem as impressive as what somebody else has. You may not have the talent, the looks, the personality, the income, or the influence that they have. But consider that what God has given you has been custom-made for you alone. He put in you exactly what you need to fulfill His plan for your life.

Today's Prayer

Heavenly Father, thank You that what You have given me is custom-made for me alone. Thank You that You have matched me for what You want me to do in my world. I believe and declare that I have exactly what I need to fulfill Your plan for my life. I declare that in my walk of faith with You, the sound of my footsteps will multiply and bring victory into my life. In Jesus' Name. Amen.

Today's Thought

God specifically gave you your gifts, your talents, your looks, and your personality. It wasn't a random happening. God didn't close His eyes and say, "Here, just take this. It will do." No, God matched you for your world.

Be Confident in Who You Are

Scripture Reading: Genesis 6

He picked up five smooth stones from a stream and put them into his shepherd's bag. Then, armed only with his shepherd's staff and sling, he started across the valley to fight the Philistine.

1 SAMUEL 17:40 NLT

A few years ago I was speaking to several hundred pastors. Afterward we had a time for questions. One pastor who stood up was about six feet five inches tall and three hundred pounds. I am five feet nine inches tall. Television makes you look bigger than you really are. He said very dramatically, "Joel, I just want to know, how much do you weigh?" I smiled and said, "I'm one hundred and fifty pounds of pure steel!"

You have to be confident in who God made you to be. You're not too short. You're not too tall. You're the right size. You have the right personality. You're the right nationality. You've been custom-made by the Creator of the universe. You have exactly what you need for where you are.

When David went out to face Goliath, King Saul tried to get David to wear his armor. David didn't have any protection, and his only weapon was his slingshot. Saul had good intentions. He said, "David, at least wear my armor. You're going to go out there and get killed." However, David was much smaller than King Saul, and when he put that armor on, it swallowed him. It didn't help him. It weighed him down. That's because what God has given other people is not going to work for you. Don't try to be like somebody else. "I wish I had their talent, their looks, their personality." If you put that armor on, you would be uncomfortable, just as David was. It would slow you down. Why? It wasn't designed for you. You are unique. You are one of a kind. God has custom-made your armor. You are wearing designer armor. Nobody has what you have. When you go out today, you need to walk with some swag!

Get up every morning and remind yourself, "I have the strength, the talent, the friends, the resources, and the qualifications I need for today." If you'll do that, because your trust is in the Lord, I believe and declare you will never lack any good thing. God is going to take the small and turn it into much. He is going to multiply what you have and take you places you've never dreamed possible.

Today's Prayer

Father, thank You that just as David did not need Saul's armor, I don't need to try to be like anyone else. Thank You that no one else has exactly what You've given me and it fits me perfectly. I believe that in You I have everything I need for where I am today.
In Jesus' Name. Amen.

Today's Thought

All David had was the slingshot. The difference was that the slingshot was a part of David's divine destiny. If he had looked at it and thought, *It's nothing. It's small. It's insignificant. I can't do this,* he would have missed his destiny.

Keep Your Crown

The Crown of Glory and Honor

Scripture Reading: Psalm 8

*You have made them a little lower than the angels
and crowned them with glory and honor.*

PSALM 8:5

When God breathed His life into you, He put a crown of glory and honor on your head. This crown represents your authority. It represents God's blessing and favor on your life. It's a reminder that you're not average, you're not mediocre: You are royalty. When you're wearing your crown, you'll have a sense of entitlement, thinking, *I have a right to be blessed. I have a right to live in victory—not because I'm so great, so strong, or so talented, but because I'm wearing a crown of honor put there by my Creator.*

Your perception of yourself will determine what kind of life you live. If you think of yourself as being average, if you feel less-than because of what somebody has said about you, if you live with guilt and condemnation because of past mistakes, that's going to limit your potential. What's happening? You're not wearing your crown.

Jesus said, "Hold on to what you have, so that no one will take your crown" (Rev. 3:11). Throughout life, there will always be someone or something trying to take your crown. People will talk about you, trying to make you look bad, to push you down. What they're really doing is trying to take your crown. Do yourself a favor. Don't let them have it. Nobody can take your crown. You have to let go of what was said or done to you rather than let go of your crown.

When thoughts tell you that you're not attractive enough, just think a better thought and say, "No, thanks. You're not taking my crown. I know I am fearfully and wonderfully made." *You'll never get out of debt.* "No, thanks. I will lend and not borrow. Whatever I touch will prosper and succeed." You're not just being positive, you're holding on to your crown. Thoughts say, *Look at where you are in life. You should be ashamed of yourself. Look at the mistakes you've made. How many times have you failed?* "No, you're not having my crown. I may have fallen, but look at me now. I didn't stay down. I got back up again. I made mistakes, but that didn't change my name. I'm still a child of the Most High God."

Today's Prayer
Father in heaven, thank You that You have put a crown of glory and honor on my head by Your grace. Thank You that I am not less-than others or just average, but You have made me royalty. I declare I will not allow anyone or anything to take my crown. In Jesus' Name. Amen.

Today's Thought
Eleanor Roosevelt said, "No one can make you feel inferior without your permission." If you're going to keep your crown, you have to dig your heels in and say, "I'm not going to let what somebody said, or the fact that someone walked away, or that something didn't work out steal my sense of value. I know I have been crowned with honor."

DAY 2

The Crown Belongs to You

Scripture Reading: Revelation 3

For if, by the trespass of the one man, death reigned
through that one man, how much more will those
who receive God's abundant provision of grace and
of the gift of righteousness reign in life through
the one man, Jesus Christ!

ROMANS 5:17

When somebody tries to make you feel small, they make derogatory statements. Instead of being upset and believing what they say, just reach up and straighten your crown. They can't change who you are unless you allow them to. They don't control your destiny. They don't determine your value. They didn't breathe life into you; God did. He calls you a masterpiece. He says you're a king, a queen. You're supposed to reign in life. That's why He put the crown of honor on your head. It's to remind you of who you are.

The mistake we make too often is to believe the lies. Somebody says, "You're not that talented." Instead of saying, "No, thanks," we say, "Oh, you're right. Let me take off my crown. I thought I was talented." The message comes to us: "You're not royalty. You come from the wrong family. You'll never do anything great." Instead of ignoring it, not giving it the time of day, we think, *What was I thinking? Let me take off my crown.*

What am I saying? People don't determine your destiny. They don't know what's in you. Don't take off your crown because somebody judged you by what they saw on the outside. Somebody told you that you're not talented enough, not attractive enough, not tall enough, not smart enough. You don't have to have them cheering you on. Keep your crown on, keep being your best, keep honoring God, and He will get you to where you're supposed to be.

The enemy's main tool is deception. There's nothing he would love more than for you to go through life not wearing your crown, letting people and circumstances convince you that "You don't deserve to be blessed. You don't have what it takes. You've been through too much. You can't feel good about yourself." Don't you dare give away your crown! It belongs to you. It was put there by your Creator. It has nothing to do with how you feel, how you look, or what other people say. It's based solely on the fact that you are a child of the Almighty God. He has crowned you with glory and honor.

Today's Prayer

Father, thank You for Your abundant provision of grace so that I might reign in life through Jesus Christ. Thank You that the crown of honor has nothing to do with how I feel or what others say. I believe it is mine as the gift of righteousness. In Jesus' Name. Amen.

Today's Thought

Has a disappointment, a bad break, or a divorce caused you to lose your passion for life? Your crown is waiting for you. Start dreaming again. Start believing again. Start hoping again.

DAY 3

Take Back Your Crown

Scripture Reading: 1 Samuel 1

*"I [Hannah] prayed for this child [Samuel],
and the L*ORD *has granted me what I asked of him.
So now I give him to the L*ORD*. For his whole life
he will be given over to the L*ORD*."*

1 SAMUEL 1:27–28

I know a young man who loved to play baseball. It was his passion growing up, but when he tried out for the school team, the coach didn't give him any chance. He said, "I'm sorry, son. You can't try out. You're too small. You could never make this team." The coach wasn't trying to be rude. He was just looking at it in the natural. But just because somebody doesn't believe in you doesn't mean that has to stop your dream.

This young man went home from school that day very discouraged; his heart was set on playing baseball. But instead of sitting around defeated, thinking he wasn't good enough, he kept his crown on. His attitude was, *The coach may say I'm too small, but I know I'm not a mistake. I'm the right size. I have what I need to fulfill my destiny.* A couple weeks later, the school announced that because so many boys had tried out for the baseball team, they were forming a second team. He tried out and made that team. He was excited about playing, even though he knew he was on the "lesser talented" team. Those two teams from the same school played in the same division with ten other teams and ended up playing each other for the championship. This young man was the pitcher on the "lesser talented" team. Although he had been told he was too small, he struck out batter after batter. They went on to beat the "more talented" team and won the division championship.

The reason people don't always encourage and cheer you on is because they can't feel what you feel. God didn't put the dream in them; He put the dream in you. Don't let their discouragement steal your enthusiasm. Keep your crown on. Keep believing. Keep hoping. Keep pursuing. You don't need everyone to be for you. You and God are a majority. When you're wearing your crown, God will open doors that no man can shut. He wouldn't have put the dream in you if He didn't already have a way to bring it to pass.

Today's Prayer
Heavenly Father, thank You that You overcame all the discouragement that Hannah experienced and she took back her crown, and I can as well in my life. Help me to keep believing, hoping, and pursuing. I believe that You will open doors that no one can shut. In Jesus' Name. Amen.

Today's Thought
Have you let a mistake, a failure, or a bankruptcy convince you to settle for second best? You need to take back your crown. You wouldn't be alive unless God had another victory in front of you. He'll help you accomplish what you could not accomplish on your own.

DAY 4

Approval Seekers

Scripture Reading: John 5

"Your approval means nothing to me…"

JOHN 5:41 NLT

Jesus said to His critics, "Your approval or disapproval means nothing to Me." That's a powerful way to live. He was saying, "I know who I am, and nothing you do or don't do is going to change it. You can celebrate Me or you can crucify Me, but I'm keeping My crown." People are impulsive. One moment they can be cheering for you, and another moment they can be putting you down, trying to make you look bad. One moment Jesus was riding a donkey into Jerusalem and the people were waving palm branches, celebrating His arrival as though He was a king. A few days later, those same people were hollering, "Crucify Him! He doesn't deserve to live!"

If wearing your crown is based on whether or not people like you, whether or not they believe in you, you're going to be taking your crown off and then putting it back on throughout your whole life. You don't need other people's approval; you have Almighty God's approval. Our attitude should be, *You can be for me or against me, you can celebrate me or criticize me, but one thing is for certain: I'm not giving you my crown. I know who I am. I am royalty. I am accepted. I am approved. I am valuable.*

In the Scripture, Isaac said to his son Esau, "Your brother has carried away your blessing." Sometimes we let other people carry away our blessing. We let what they say about us—their disapproval and discouraging words—keep us from who we were meant to be. You have to put your foot down and say, "I'm not going to let people talk me out of my dreams. I'm not going to let a coworker make me feel inferior, as though I'm not good enough. I'm not going to let a coach, a teacher, or a counselor talk me into living an average, mediocre, get-by life." You have seeds of greatness. You are destined to leave your mark on this generation. Don't let anyone carry away your blessing.

Today's Prayer
Father, thank You that I do not need to be concerned about whether or not people like me or believe in me. Thank You that Your approval is all that I need. I believe that I am accepted by, approved by, and valuable to You, and I refuse to allow others to carry away my blessing. In Jesus' Name. Amen.

Today's Thought
Before you were formed in your mother's womb, God knew you and He approved you. When God made you, He stepped back and said, "I like that. That was good. Another masterpiece!" He stamped His approval on you. You are not lacking anything.

Where the Negative Thoughts Come From

Scripture Reading: Genesis 3

But I am afraid that just as Eve was deceived by the serpent's cunning, your minds may somehow be led astray from your sincere and pure devotion to Christ.

2 CORINTHIANS 11:3

When we look back, we can see that the enemy's been trying to get our crown from the beginning of time. In the Garden of Eden, Adam and Eve were living confident and secure. They were at peace with God, at peace with themselves. They were wearing their crowns. They knew they had God's blessing and favor. But one day the enemy deceived them into eating the forbidden fruit. When they did, immediately they were afraid. They ran and hid. In effect, they gave the enemy their crowns.

That's what happens when we surrender our crown of honor. It opens the door to fear, insecurity, and shame. We focus on what we're not, on the mistakes we've made, on what other people have said about us. Where there's no crown, there's no covering. There's no reminder of who we are. We believe those lies that can push us down.

When God came looking for Adam and Eve, He called out to Adam, "Where are you?" Adam said, "We're hiding because we're naked." God asked, "Who told you that you were naked?" God knew Adam had taken off his crown. God is asking us today, "Who told you you're just average? That you can't accomplish your dreams? That you come from the wrong family? That you're not good enough?" I can assure you those negative thoughts didn't come from our God. You need to put your crown back on. You may have let some person or some event take it. The good news is that you can get it back. It's not too late; you have control over your crown.

It starts in your thinking. No more "I'm just a C student. I'm just average." Say, "I am an A student. I will excel in school." When you think better, you live better. No more "I lost a loved one. I'll never be happy again." Say, "God is giving me beauty for these ashes. What He started in my life, He will finish." Don't sit around feeling sorry for yourself. Put your crown back on. No more "I come from the wrong family. There's nothing special about me." Say, "I've been made in the image of Almighty God. I'm a masterpiece, one of a kind. I am a prized possession."

Today's Prayer
Father in heaven, thank You that You gave me the crown
of honor and even the enemy does not have the power
to take it from me. Thank You that I am covered by
Your grace and favor, that I am made in Your image.
I believe that I will reach my highest potential.
In Jesus' Name. Amen.

Today's Thought
If you're going to reach your highest potential, you
have to keep your crown on and say, "I have the favor
of God. I am equipped, empowered, and anointed."
It doesn't happen automatically. That's why the
Scripture says to hold fast to what you have so
that no one takes it away.

DAY 6

Think Like Royalty, Live Like Royalty

Scripture Reading: Isaiah 61

...to bestow on them a crown of beauty instead of ashes, the oil of joy instead of mourning, and a garment of praise instead of a spirit of despair. They will be called oaks of righteousness, a planting of the LORD for the display of his splendor.

ISAIAH 61:3

I talked to a young lady recently who was very discouraged because her husband left her for someone else. She was a beautiful woman, but now she was convinced that she wasn't attractive enough, talented enough, or smart enough. She had given her crown away. She told me all the things she should have done better. "If I'd only done this, if I'd only done that." In her mind, it was all her fault. But when somebody leaves your life, it doesn't necessarily mean there's something wrong with you. It could be the other person has the problem. Nevertheless, the accuser will work overtime trying to convince you that you don't measure up, that you're not valuable, and that there's nothing good in your future. He's trying to take your crown.

The Scripture says God will never leave us or forsake us. If they left you and you needed them, that would mean God was forsaking you. So you can conclude that if they left, you didn't need them. If they walked away, they weren't a part of your destiny. Isaiah said God will give you double for the unfair things that have happened. You may not realize it, but when they left, in a sense, they set you up for what God really wants to do.

He has somebody amazing in your future! A divine connection. Somebody better than you could imagine. Somebody who will treat you like the king, the queen, you were meant to be. But you have to do your part and put your crown back on. It's not going to happen if you go around negative, discouraged, and feeling unattractive. If you feel unattractive on the inside, you'll be unattractive on the outside. You carry yourself the way you feel about yourself.

When you're wearing your crown, you are confident and secure. You know you're a masterpiece, one of a kind, a prized possession. You're not dwelling on all the negative chatter—what you're not, what you don't have, or what other people are saying. You go through the day with a smile on your face and a spring in your step. You know you're royalty, that you've been crowned with glory and honor.

Today's Prayer
Father, thank You that You will never leave me or forsake me. Thank You that You have a way of restoring to me double for the unfair things that have happened to me. I believe that You will always give me a crown of beauty instead of ashes and the oil of joy instead of mourning. In Jesus' Name. Amen.

———

Today's Thought
When you think like royalty, you will live like royalty, and you're going to come into divine connections. You won't have to go after them. God will cause the right people to track you down.

Payback Is Coming

Scripture Reading: Ruth 4

The women said to Naomi: "Praise be to the Lord, who this day has not left you without a guardian-redeemer.… He will renew your life and sustain you in your old age."

RUTH 4:14–15

Naomi had first lost her husband in death, and then both her married sons died as well. She was so discouraged she didn't think she could go on. She took off her crown. She had been full of joy and sweetness, but now she was bitter. She even changed her name from Naomi, which means "my joy," to Mara, which means "bitter." When people called her Naomi, she would say, "Please don't call me that. Call me bitter." The problem is that when you take off your crown, you also take off the favor, the honor, and the glory, those things you need for God to pay you back.

Naomi thought her life was finished. But when she saw some old friends and tried to persuade them to call her Mara, they said, "Naomi, that's not who you are. We're calling you, 'My joy.'" They kept calling her Naomi. Every time they did, they were prophesying her future. She was trying to stay in defeat, but they said, "No, you're coming into victory." She kept taking her crown off, and they kept putting it back on.

You need people around you who will remind you about who you are. Stay close to people who will call you blessed, call you victorious, call you royalty. You want people in your life who will remind you that your best days are yet to come, that what was meant for your harm, God will use to your advantage—people who will help you keep your crown on.

When Naomi's widowed daughter-in-law Ruth met a man named Boaz, they married. One day they had a little baby boy. It hadn't seemed as though Naomi had any reason to live, but when she saw that little baby, something came alive on the inside. The Scripture says, "The women in the town rejoiced, saying, 'Naomi, this baby will restore your youth.'" She felt a new sense of purpose. She took care of that little baby as though he were her own. Naomi thought she'd never be happy again, but now she was more fulfilled than ever. That was God paying her back for the unfair things that had happened—she had her crown back on.

Today's Prayer

Heavenly Father, thank You that You are able to take the most unfair situations in my life and turn them into wonderful positives. And thank You for the people in my life who help me keep my crown on. Help me to stay close to those who remind me about who I am, a child of the King over all, the Almighty God. In Jesus' Name. Amen.

Today's Thought

Are you wearing your crown today? Or have you let a disappointment, a loss, or a bad break convince you to take it off? In the tough times, more than ever, you need to keep reminding yourself, "I am a child of the Most High God. He has beauty for these ashes; double is coming my way."

Rediscover Who You Are

Scripture Reading: Psalm 105

Look to the LORD and his strength; seek his face always.
Remember the wonders he has done, his miracles,
and the judgments he pronounced.

PSALM 105:4–5

I heard a version of the mythological story about Helen of Troy. She was an extremely beautiful queen, a young woman born into royalty, loved and admired by all the people. But one day she was kidnapped and taken away to a foreign country. With all the confusion, she was stricken with amnesia. She couldn't remember her name or where she was from. She ended up living on the streets, homeless, being taken advantage of. Nobody knew where she was and she didn't know who she was. Back at home, even as the years passed, her friends and family believed she was still alive. Then one man who loved her dearly set out to try to find her.

While he was searching the streets of a faraway country, he saw a pitiful-looking woman whose clothes were ragged, hair was matted, and face was battered. But she looked strangely familiar to him. The man asked her what her name was. She mumbled something and wouldn't really talk. He looked closer and asked if he could see her hands. He remembered the line prints on Helen's hands. When the woman showed him her hands, he couldn't believe it. He whispered, "Helen." She looked at him, confused. He said, "You are Helen of Troy. You are the queen. Helen, don't you remember?" Suddenly her face brightened and the fog lifted.

She rediscovered who she really was, and once again she became the queen she was meant to be.

Similar to Helen, too many people today are suffering from spiritual amnesia. They were born into royalty, created to reign in life. God crowned them with honor and glory, but they've somehow forgotten who they are. Because of bad breaks, disappointments, and the mistakes they've made, they feel beaten down by life and are living far below their privileges, thinking that they're average. As this man did for Helen, I'm here to remind you of whose you are. You are a child of the Most High God. You have royal blood flowing through your veins. There is a crown of honor that belongs to you. Now do your part and put your crown back on and live royally.

Today's Prayer

Father, thank You that You are always there to help me put my crown back on after I've taken it off. Thank You that I can bring to remembrance the wonders You have done in my life. I declare that I am Your child with royal blood flowing in my veins. In Jesus' Name. Amen.

Today's Thought

Nothing that's happened to you has stopped God's plan. He knows how to give beauty for ashes, how to turn mourning into dancing. Strongholds that have held you back are being broken. The chains of defeated thinking and a negative mentality are being loosed. You're going to rediscover who you really are. You are not average or mediocre; you are royalty—a king, a queen.

Keep Your Blessing

Scripture Reading: Daniel 3

*Nebuchadnezzar said, "Praise be to the God of Shadrach,
Meshach and Abednego, who has sent his angel and
rescued his servants! They trusted in him and defied the
king's command and were willing to give up
their lives rather than serve or worship any
god except their own God."*

DANIEL 3:28

I read about an eight-year-old boy who was born a few years before the French Revolution. His father was King Louis XVI. During all the violent insurrection, first the boy's entire family was imprisoned, and then both his mother and father were condemned to death. In January 1793, his father was brought out to the public square and beheaded, and his mother suffered the same fate the following October. The young prince remained a threat to the leaders of the revolution, who determined to "retrain" Louis XVII to make him compliant to the revolution and to accuse his mother of wrongdoing. Stories circulated that the royal heir to the throne was subjected to extreme cruelty, and attempts were made to teach him to say profane things, to lie, to cheat, and to do wrong. While no one knows exactly what happened, in my imagination I can see him putting his foot down when they tried to make him speak in profanities and saying, "No, I'm not going to do it. I was born to be a king. I will not talk that way." When they tried to get him to lie, to cheat, to compromise, the same thing: "I am a king. I will not do it."

When the enemy tries to reprogram your thinking, telling

you that you're average, you're ordinary, just say, "No, thanks. I'm a king. I will not think that way." When thoughts try to convince you to live a mediocre, defeated life, say, "No, thanks. I know I am royalty. I will not live beneath my privileges. I know I am a child of the Most High God."

I'm asking you to keep your crown on. You may have been through disappointments and loss. Life will try to take it. You have to hold fast to what God has given you. Don't let anyone or anything carry away your blessing. If you'll make this decision with me that you're going to keep your crown on, I believe and declare you will reign in life, rise higher, accomplish your dreams, and reach the fullness of your destiny.

Today's Prayer

Father in heaven, thank You for the example of Shadrach, Meshach, and Abednego, who refused to take off their crowns. Thank You that I can hold fast to what You've given me and walk in Your blessing. I will not live beneath my privileges as Your child. In Jesus' Name. Amen.

Today's Thought

Put your crown back on. That crown is what gives you the favor. Nothing that's happened has lessened your value. You are the prized possession, the apple of God's eye. Don't let a disappointment or a loss carry away your blessing. It's not the end. It's a new beginning.

Just
Remember

It Was the Hand of God

Scripture Reading: Psalm 103

Praise the LORD, my soul, and forget not all his benefits—
who forgives all your sins and heals all your diseases,
who redeems your life from the pit and crowns
you with love and compassion...

PSALM 103:2–4

When you look back over your life, consider some of the things you've faced that at the time you didn't think you could make it through. The obstacle was so large, the breakup hurt you so badly, the medical report was so negative. You didn't see a way, but God turned it around. He gave you strength when you didn't think you could go on. He brought the right person when you needed them. He promoted you, gave you that good break, and things fell into place. Now you're further along than you ever imagined.

That wasn't a lucky break. It wasn't a coincidence. It was the hand of God. You should have been stuck, addicted, broke, depressed, and lonely, but God made a way when you didn't see a way. You can say what I say: "I didn't get to where I am by myself. It wasn't just my good luck, my hard work, or my talent. It was the favor of God. He made things happen that I could never make happen on my own."

But none of us like difficulties. If we had a choice, we wouldn't go through them. However, those challenges not only prepared you for your future, but now you have a history with God. When you're in a tough time, and you don't see a way out, instead of being discouraged and negative, you can remember how God turned your health around. Remember how He gave you that baby when the specialist said you couldn't have a child. Remember how He brought you out of that trouble that you got yourself into.

When you remember how God has protected you, promoted you, healed you, and restored you, faith will rise in your heart. Instead of thinking, *I'll never get out of this problem*, you'll say with confidence, "God made a way in the past; I know He's going to make a way in the future." Don't complain about the problem. It's not random. You're going to need that victory in the future. God is taking you from glory to glory. When you come through this challenge, that victory will be the fuel you use that gets you to the next level of glory.

Today's Prayer

Father, thank You that Your hand has been upon my life in so many ways. Thank You for the countless things You have made happen for my good and Your glory that I could never make happen on my own. I believe You are protecting me, promoting me, healing me, and restoring me. In Jesus' Name. Amen.

Today's Thought

When you're constantly thinking about God's goodness, how He's protected you, vindicated you, and promoted you, not only will faith rise in your heart, but it's that attitude of expectancy that allows God to do great things in your future.

DAY 2

Develop the Habit of Remembering

Scripture Reading: Deuteronomy 8

You may say to yourselves, "These nations are stronger than we are. How can we drive them out?" But do not be afraid of them; remember well what the LORD your God did to Pharaoh and to all Egypt.

DEUTERONOMY 7:17–18

This is what happened with the Israelites. They were up against huge armies, against nations that were stronger, had more equipment, and were more skilled in warfare. The Israelites had just come out of slavery. They had no military training or weapons; they were just trying to survive in the desert. They were headed toward the Promised Land, but they had one enemy after another to overcome. They were very discouraged. They didn't know how they could do it.

God said to them, "You may think, 'How can we conquer these nations that are much stronger than us?' But don't be afraid. Just remember what God did to Pharaoh. You saw with your own eyes the miraculous signs and the amazing power God used to bring you out." God was saying, "When it looks impossible, when you don't see a way out, the way to stay encouraged and keep your hopes up is to remember what God has done."

As was true for the Israelites, we have seen with our own eyes those times when God made a way. You thought you were stuck, but God opened a door. He caused somebody to be good to you. You faced the loss of a loved one, and you thought you would never be happy again, but God lifted you out of that pit. He turned your mourning into dancing.

If you're going to overcome obstacles, if you're going to reach your highest potential, you have to learn to remember. On a regular basis, we should go back over the major victories in our life. Remember how He put you at the right place at the right time and you met that person and fell in love. Remember how He spared your life from that accident. Remember how the medical report said you shouldn't be here, but you are alive, strong, and healthy today. Remember the day your child was born. Remember how God gave you that job, how He protected you, and how you met the right person.

Develop this habit of remembering what God has done. These are the better thoughts that will propel you forward in the future.

Today's Prayer

Heavenly Father, thank You for the strength and hope that rise within me whenever I remember all that You have done in my life. Thank You for the countless times You made a way when it seemed there was no way and You opened doors that seemed closed. I will not be afraid, I will trust in You. In Jesus' Name. Amen.

Today's Thought

When you face tough times and your dream looks impossible, every voice says, "It's never going to happen." Just remember. Go back and replay your victories. Relive the times God made a way.

DAY 3

The Mercies of God

Scripture Reading: Psalm 51

I appeal to you therefore, brothers, by the mercies
of God, to present your bodies as a living sacrifice,
holy and acceptable to God, which is
your spiritual worship.

ROMANS 12:1 ESV

When the apostle Paul talks about "the mercies of God" in the Scripture, he doesn't use the singular but the plural. Every one of us has experienced some of these mercies.

When I was first married, I was driving on the freeway during a big rainstorm and lost control of my car. I started spinning around and around, crossing the different lanes of the freeway. At one point I looked up and saw this eighteen-wheeler coming right at me. At that moment, I was going in the wrong direction. We were so close I felt as though I could touch his front grille, and I thought, *That's it. I'm done.* All I could say was "Jesus!" When you're in that kind of trouble, you don't have to pray long. Somehow that big truck missed me, and the driver pulled his big rig over. He got out of his cab, walked over to my car, and when he looked into my window at me, his eyes were very big. He said, "I can't believe I didn't run over you, but at the last second a big gust of wind blew my truck into the other lane." He said it was the wind; I know it was the mercies of God.

When our son, Jonathan, was less than a year old, we were on a boat with some friends. He was in the baby carrier, and we'd set it on the bench in the boat. As we were traveling along, something whispered to Victoria, "Go hold on to your son." She walked over and held on to the baby carrier. About thirty seconds later, the boat hit a huge wave and everything that wasn't tied down went flying overboard. Jonathan would have been thrown into the water if not for the mercies of God.

Many of you can join me in saying that you wouldn't be alive if it wasn't for God's mercies. Some of the things you've done—the crowds you used to run with, the drugs, the alcohol, the reckless driving, the freak accidents—should have taken you out. But God showed you some of His mercies—not once, but again and again.

Today's Prayer

Father, thank You for all of the times when You've shown me such great mercy. Thank You for how You've protected me from accidents and delivered me from dangers and mistakes I've made. Your mercies have freed me from sin. I declare that it is Your mercies that keep me safe every day. In Jesus' Name. Amen.

Today's Thought

You're not just lucky; you don't just keep beating the odds. It's the mercies of God. In fact, the reason you're still here, the reason that truck couldn't run over you, the reason those drugs couldn't kill you, the reason the sickness couldn't take you out is because God has a destiny for you to fulfill. He has an assignment for you to accomplish.

DAY 4

Recognize What God Has Done

Scripture Reading: Psalm 57

Have mercy on me, my God, have mercy on me,
for in you I take refuge. I will take refuge in
the shadow of your wings...

PSALM 57:1

I remember in my early twenties when I walked into a jewelry store to buy a battery for my watch. I was simply minding my own business when out walked the most beautiful girl I'd ever seen. It was Victoria. I recognize that encounter wasn't a coincidence. That wasn't a lucky break. That was God directing my steps, putting me at the right place at the right time, and He used a battery to do it. When I think about that, it reminds me how God is in control of my life. If He was directing my steps back then, I know He's directing my steps right now.

Maybe you shouldn't have the position you're in at your workplace. You weren't the most qualified, but the mercies of God gave it to you. Or perhaps that sickness said it was going to be the end, but the mercies of God said, "This is not your time." When you recognize what God has done, that all through your life it's been His hand getting you to where you are, then it's easy to honor God. It's easy to be grateful. It's easy to serve, to give, and to help others. You realize that where you are in life is because of the mercies of God.

You know you're driving a mercy car. You're living in a mercy house. You're working at a mercy job. You didn't just marry over your head, you married mercy. Maybe you felt you were about to have a nervous breakdown, but mercy showed up. You should be depressed, but mercy turned you around. You could be in prison, but mercy kept you out. Perhaps you even tried to take your own life, but mercy kept you alive. Mercy gave you that baby. Mercy gave you that idea. Mercy opened that door. Don't take it for granted. Keep it in the forefront of your mind.

You might as well recognize you're a marked man, a marked woman. The Creator of the universe has His hand on your life. The sooner you surrender your will to His, the better off you're going to be. You're not giving up anything. You're gaining purpose, your destiny, a life that He's designed, a life more rewarding than you ever imagined.

Today's Prayer

Father in heaven, thank You that in Your love You chose me before I chose You. Help me to keep Your mercies in the forefront of my mind. I surrender my will to You, and I believe that You are leading me forward into the life that You designed for me. In Jesus' Name. Amen.

Today's Thought

God's mercies are never going to give up on you. His calling is irrevocable. He chose you before you could choose Him. You love Him because He first loved you.

The Goodness of God

Scripture Reading: Psalm 129

[What, what would have become of me]
had I not believed that I would see
the Lord's goodness in the land
of the living!

PSALM 27:13 AMPC

In today's verse, David was saying in effect, "If God had not shown me some of His goodness, I wouldn't have defeated Goliath or outlasted King Saul when he was trying to kill me in the desert. I wouldn't have been restored after my mistake with Bathsheba without God's mercy."

A young man told me how he was partying with some friends and accidentally got several different types of drugs mixed up. He took so many that his friends thought for sure he would pass out or have convulsions. But those drugs had no effect on him. It was as though they had lost all their power. He said, "Joel, I'm one lucky guy." I told him it's a lot more than luck; it's the mercies of God.

Psalm 129 says, "From my earliest youth my enemies have persecuted me, but they have never been able to finish me off." Sometimes you need to just thank God that you're still here. Cancer and depression couldn't finish you off. That divorce, the legal problems, the bankruptcy couldn't finish you off. Perhaps the naysayers tried to push you down, doing their best to make you look bad, but their best was not powerful enough. They couldn't finish you off. You got knocked down, but you got back up again. You had a setback or a breakup, but you're still in the game. You went through a loss, but you didn't get bitter, you kept moving forward.

When my father was a little boy, he fell into a large fire that should have taken his life, but the fire could not finish him off. He was raised during the Great Depression with next to nothing, but poverty could not finish him off. His first marriage as a young man didn't make it, but divorce couldn't finish him off. Years later, some people turned on him and asked him to leave his church, but betrayal couldn't finish him off. He had high blood pressure most of his life, but that couldn't finish him off.

God is called the author and the finisher of our faith. What He started in your life, He will finish—not a bad break, not a disappointment, not a sickness. God is the finisher.

Today's Prayer
Father, thank You that You are the author and finisher
of my faith. Thank You that all that comes against me
to defeat me cannot finish me off because You raise up a
barrier to protect me. I believe that You will bring
to a finish the work You are doing in my life.
In Jesus' Name. Amen.

Today's Thought
God has the final say. People can't finish you off. A bad
break, betrayal, rejection, or sickness can't do it. When the
enemy comes in like a flood, the Scripture says God raises
up a barrier. God will put a stop to it. The forces that are
for you are greater than the forces that are against you.

What You Don't Even Know About

Scripture Reading: John 10

*"I give them eternal life, and they shall never perish;
no one will snatch them out of my hand. My Father,
who has given them to me, is greater than all; no one
can snatch them out of my Father's hand."*

JOHN 10:28–29

You may be in a difficult time. Don't get discouraged. Just remember the Red Seas that God has already parted in your life. Remember how God delivered you from the Pharaoh, so to speak. He snatched you out of a harmful situation. He closed that door that would have proven a big mistake. You have a history with God. You've seen His mercies—not once, but again and again—showing out in your life.

You need to announce to that cancer, "You can't finish me off. The God who spoke worlds into existence controls the number of my days." Announce to that depression, fear, and anxiety, "You're not going to finish me off. God promised I will finish my course with joy." Don't get discouraged because of that person who's trying to push you down and make you look bad. They don't control your destiny. They can't stop God's plan for your life. When negative thoughts come, just answer back, "You don't realize who you're dealing with. I'm a child of the Most High God. You cannot finish me off."

In the New Testament days, Saul was one of the greatest enemies of the church. He was headed straight toward Damascus with authority to arrest any followers of Christ. The believers in Damascus didn't even know it. He was going to cause them tremendous heartache and pain. It looked inevitable. But suddenly a bright light shone down on Saul from heaven. The light was so strong it knocked him to the ground. In a split second, God stopped the persecutor in his tracks…and in the process changed him into an apostle.

We all need to realize there were times in our past when we knew nothing about it, but something was coming our way—a bad break, an accident, a sickness. It should have finished us off, but God said, "No, I don't think so. That's My son, that's My daughter. I'm putting a stop to it." An eighteen-wheeler should've finished me off, but God pushed the truck out of the way. There have been many things you knew nothing about, but God stopped a cancer, stopped a betrayal, or stopped a rejection. It was all behind the scenes. That's the mercies of God.

Today's Prayer

Heavenly Father, thank You that You control the number of my days and nothing can stop Your plan for my life. Thank You for the countless ways that You have protected me from things I knew nothing about. I rejoice that Your mercies surround me. In Jesus' Name. Amen.

Today's Thought

You need to thank God for what didn't happen in your life. Thank Him for the enemies He stopped that you know nothing about.

DAY 7

Remember the Right Things

Scripture Reading: 1 Chronicles 29

"Yours, O LORD, is the greatness, the power, the glory, the victory, and the majesty. Everything in the heavens and on earth is yours, O LORD, and this is your kingdom. We adore you as the one who is over all things."

1 CHRONICLES 29:11 NLT

You may be saying, "Joel, this sounds encouraging, but I've had a lot of bad breaks and gone through a lot of disappointments. I didn't get the promotion for which I worked so hard. This person walked out of my life." Here's the problem: You're remembering the wrong things. I can't find one place in the Scripture where we're told to remember our defeats, remember our failures, or remember our bad breaks. "Well, my company laid me off twenty-seven years ago. It wasn't right." May I tell you this respectfully? It's time to get over it. Quit thinking about it, quit talking about it, and quit reliving it. All that it's doing is depressing you. Has God done anything good for you in the last twenty-seven years? Have you seen one promotion, one healing, one sign of His favor?

Start remembering your victories, the times God healed you, the times He promoted you, the times He stopped the accidents, the times He turned the problems around. When you're remembering the right things, you're going to move forward in faith. You'll see more of God's favor.

David said in Psalm 34, "Let all who are discouraged take heart." He goes on to tell us how to do it. "Come, let's talk about God's goodness. I prayed and the Lord answered my prayer."

He was saying, "When you don't see a way out, come and let's talk—not about what didn't work out. No, let's talk about God's greatness. Let's talk about your answered prayers. Let's talk about the Red Seas that have been parted."

What you're saying in your tough times will make or break you. If you go around saying, "I'll never get out of this problem. It's just too big," you'll get stuck. Turn it around and say, "God, I want to thank You for Your greatness in my life. Thank You for giving me this job. Lord, thank You for freeing me from this addiction." When you're always talking about God's goodness, you won't be down and discouraged. You'll have a spring in your step, a smile on your face. You'll know that God has done it for you in the past, and He'll do it for you again in the future.

Today's Prayer

Father, You are the greatness, the power, the glory, the victory, and the majesty in my life. I believe that as I talk about Your goodness and greatness in my life, I am putting myself in position for You to do something even more amazing for Your glory, for Your kingdom, for Your honor. In Jesus' Name. Amen.

Today's Thought

When you constantly think about what God has done, when you relive your miracles, when you're always in awe of His goodness, you are putting yourself in position for God to do something even more amazing.

Mountable

Scripture Reading: Psalm 145

*Blessed are the chosen!... We expect our fill of
good things in your house, your heavenly manse.
All your salvation wonders are on display
in your trophy room.*

PSALM 65:4–5 MSG

In the home of a friend of mine, he has a large mounted sword-fish over his fireplace and a gorgeous blue marlin hanging on the wall next to his television. The first time I went into his house, we spent over an hour just going from room to room, taking in all his trophy fish. He described where and how he caught them. He's also caught a lot of small fish, but he mounted only the large fish.

In the same way, God has done many great things for us. He provides our daily needs and gives us strength, wisdom, and protection. We're grateful for His goodness. But God wants to do some things in your life that are mountable, some things that are so big, so impressive, you will want to hang them on your wall, in a manner of speaking. When people see you, you have something to point at. "This is what God did in my life."

My mother was diagnosed with terminal cancer and given a few weeks to live. Today, thirty-five years later, she's still alive, healthy and strong. Everywhere she goes she has something to talk about, something impressive, something out of the ordinary, a trophy of God's goodness. You can look back and see times when God did something unusual in your life. Maybe you shouldn't be living in the house that you're in now. You didn't have the funds, but things fell into place. You know it was the hand of God. That's mountable.

Perhaps you struggled with an addiction. You were off course, but today you're clean, you're free, you're being a blessing to others. As is true of my mother, you are a living testimony. You don't have to go look for a miracle; you are a miracle. When you need to be encouraged, just go look at yourself in the mirror. You shouldn't be where you are. Perhaps you should still be struggling, addicted, angry, depressed, and lonely, but God in His mercy showed up and said, "I don't think so." When it looked impossible, He stopped it. He's given you something to talk about. You're a trophy of God's goodness. Now here's the key: Don't let what once was a miracle become ordinary. Don't lose the awe of what God has done.

Today's Prayer
Father in heaven, thank You for all the wonders You have worked in my life. Thank You for all that I can point to and say: This is what You've done. I declare that I am a trophy of Your goodness. You have made me a miracle of Your grace. In Jesus' Name. Amen.

———

Today's Thought
Everywhere you go, talk about God's goodness—not bragging about yourself, but bragging about what God has done. God wants to give you some new things to mount. Get ready for favor that you haven't yet seen, for opportunity, influence, and promotion. He has something out of the ordinary, something impressive, a new level coming your way.

DAY 9

Consider Your History

Scripture Reading: Mark 6

...because they had not understood [the miracle of] the loaves [how it revealed the power and deity of Jesus].

MARK 6:52 AMP

On one occasion, the disciples had seen Jesus take five loaves of bread and two fish, pray over them, and feed some fifteen thousand people. Just a few hours later, they were in a boat on a lake when strong winds suddenly swept down, and the waves were very high. The disciples were concerned for their safety when they saw Jesus walking on the water. At first, in the pitch black of night, they thought He was a ghost. They finally recognized Him and invited Him into their boat. When He got into the boat, the winds and waves calmed down immediately. They were relieved they were okay.

But the Scripture gives us insight into why they were so worried. It says, "They didn't consider or understand the miracle of the loaves." They were so stressed out by the high waves, they forgot how earlier that day they had seen with their own eyes one of the greatest miracles ever recorded. If they had just remembered what God had done, they would have stayed in faith. They would have been calm, knowing that everything would be okay despite the waves. They did not remember what God had done.

Are you doing what they did? Are you letting your circumstances, a medical report, or a financial situation cause you to live worried, stressed out? Why don't you start considering your miracles? Look back over your life. Remember the time God showed up and suddenly turned it around. Look on your walls and relive some of those mountable things God has done.

How are you going to defeat the Pharaohs in your life? How are you going to overcome those large obstacles? God is saying to you what He said to the Israelites: Just remember. You have a history with God. Every victory He's given you wasn't just for that time; it was so you could go back and use that as fuel to build your faith. If you are low on faith, you need to go back and get some fuel. It's in your past victories. Don't talk about your problems; talk about the greatness of God.

Remember, the enemy cannot finish you off; God has the final say.

Today's Prayer
Father, thank You for the history that I have with You and for the mercies that You have shown out in my life. Thank You that I remember the victories You've given me and use it as fuel to build my faith. I believe You have the final say in all things. In Jesus' Name. Amen.

Today's Thought
If you'll develop this habit of just remembering, I believe and declare that God is about to show out in your life. As you think better, you're going to live better. He's going to give you something new to mount. You're going to rise higher, accomplish your dreams, go places you never thought possible.

STAY**CONNECTED,**
BE**BLESSED.**

From thoughtful articles to powerful blogs, podcasts and more, JoelOsteen.com is full of inspirations that will give you encouragement and confidence in your daily life.

AVAILABLE ON JOELOSTEEN.COM

 today's**W**O**RD**

This daily devotional from Joel and Victoria will help you grow in your relationship with the Lord and equip you to be everything God intends you to be.

Joel Osteen
STREAMING

Miss a broadcast? Watch Joel Osteen on demand, and see Joel LIVE on Sundays.

 Joel Osteen
PODCAST

The podcast is a great way to listen to Joel where you want, when you want.

CONNECT WITH US

Join our community of believers on your favorite social network.

TAKE HOPE WITH YOU

Get the inspiration and encouragement of Joel Osteen on your iPhone, iPad or Android device! Our app puts Joel's messages, devotions and more at your fingertips.

Thanks for helping us make a difference in the lives of millions around the world.

Notes

Notes

Notes